CASE STUDIES IN

CULTURAL ANTHROPOLOGY

GENERAL EDITORS

George and Louise Spindler

STANFORD UNIVERSITY

THE KONYAK NAGAS

An Indian Frontier Tribe

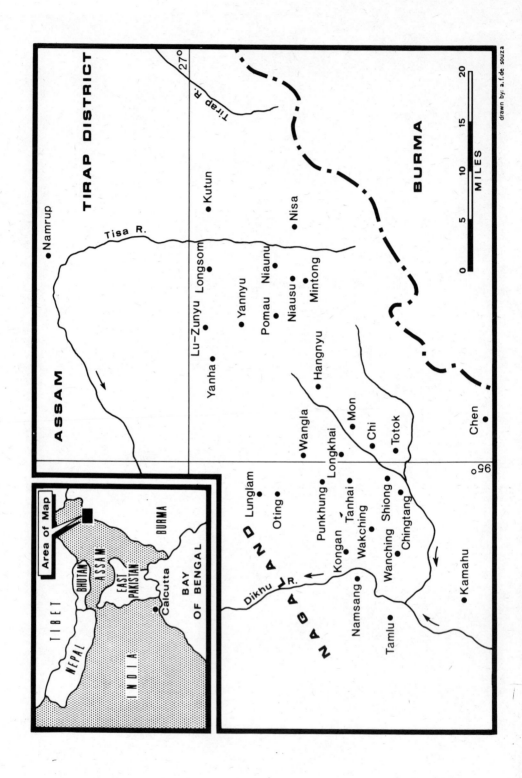

drawn by: a.f. de souza

TIRAP DISTRICT

27°

Tirap R.

ASSAM

Namrup

Tisa R.

Kutun

Nisa

Lu-Zunyu Longsom

Yannyu

Pomau Niaunu

Niausu

Mintong

Yanha

Hangnyu

Wangla

Mon

Chi

Totok

Chen

BURMA

MILES

0   5   10   15   20

96°

Lunglam

Oting

Punkhung Longkhai

Kongan Tanhai

Wakching

Wanching Shiong

Chingtang

Kamahu

Namsang

Tamlu

Dikhu R.

NAGALAND

Area of Map

TIBET

NEPAL

BHUTAN

ASSAM

EAST PAKISTAN

BURMA

INDIA

Calcutta

BAY OF BENGAL

THE KONYAK NAGAS

An Indian Frontier Tribe

By

CHRISTOPH VON FÜRER-HAIMENDORF

University of London

HOLT, RINEHART AND WINSTON

NEW YORK   CHICAGO   SAN FRANCISCO   ATLANTA

DALLAS   MONTREAL   TORONTO   LONDON   SYDNEY

Foreword

About the Series

These case studies in cultural anthropology are designed to bring to students, in beginning and intermediate courses in the social sciences, insights into the richness and complexity of human life as it is lived in different ways and in different places. They are written by men and women who have lived in the societies they write about and who are professionally trained as observers and interpreters of human behavior. The authors are also teachers, and in writing their books they have kept the students who will read them foremost in their minds. It is our belief that when an understanding of ways of life very different from one's own is gained, abstractions and generalizations about social structure, cultural values, subsistence techniques, and the other universal categories of human social behavior become meaningful.

About the Author

Christoph von Fürer-Haimendorf was born in Austria and studied anthropology at the University of Vienna and the London School of Economics and Political Science. He has held teaching positions on four continents and is now a professor of Asian anthropology and head of the Department of Anthropology and Sociology at the School of Oriental and African Studies, University of London.

In 1936–1937 he worked among the Konyak Nagas on the Assam-Burma border and subsequently he spent a total of some fifteen years in India and Nepal, partly engaged in anthropological research and partly in the service of the government of India and the government of Hyderabad in administrative positions connected with tribal affairs. In addition to the books and articles listed on page 110, his publications include *The Chenchus* (1943), *The Reddis of the Bison Hills* (1945), *The Raj Gonds* (1948), *The Sherpas of Nepal* (1964), *Caste and Kin in Nepal, India and Ceylon* (1966), and numerous contributions to symposia and periodicals.

Though the major part of his field research was concentrated on the tribes of peninsular India, and more recently on the Buddhist populations of Nepal, he has also shown a sustained interest in the peoples of the North East Frontier Agency. In 1944 and 1945 he explored the then little-known Subansiri region and his reports to the government of India laid the foundation for the ethnographic knowledge of that section of the eastern Himalayas.

About the Book

This case study is notable for the balance presented and retained between three emphases: structural analysis of group and class relationships; comparative cross-referencing of significant patterns of culture and social organization; attention to the qualitative details of interpersonal and group relationships, and of the life cycle. It is rare to find these three themes represented within a single ethnography, and more rare to find them presented so processually that the reader is never overcome with pedantic abstractions. He is led, rather, into the intimate details of life among the Konyak Nagas in such a way that the interpretation is organically and inductively integrated with the factual substance that makes it meaningful. We leave to the reader the discovery of these three themes as he is led through the rich complexity of Konyak life.

As Fürer-Haimendorf points out, he was fortunate in being able to observe the Konyak Nagas in a tradition of anthropological fieldwork that is now fast disappearing. He lived with and observed a people effectively out of contact with the modern world. At the time he did his first field study with them, in 1936–1937, the Konyak Nagas had only recently been brought under British administration. Although head-hunting had been banned in the village of Wakching, where he took up residence, its traditions and meaning were very much alive, and in nearby villages that he visited it was still practiced. Very little else in the culture, and virtually nothing in social or political organization, had been changed as the result of British administration or by the trading forays into the lower plains inhabited by people dominated by Hindu civilization. This case study therefore brings to the series representation of a widespread archaic culture in an intact state that lies wholly outside of Hindu culture and ideology and that is distinct from the peasant economies of the historic civilizations of southeast Asia. An additional dimension is added to the study through Fürer-Haimendorf's recent visit, in 1962, to a district inhabited by a people culturally indistinguishable from the Konyak Nagas, and only 20 miles distant from the site of his earlier study. This is most fortunate, for no anthropological fieldwork has been possible in Nagaland since the independence of India due to the turbulent political situation in that area. Fürer-Haimendorf is able to bring into focus some of the significant forces for change, and some of the reasons for Naga resistance to the new administration and for the continuing demands by the Naga for independence.

Given the richness of Naga culture, and the richness of this case study, one could pick out many focuses for attention in an introductory comment. Of the many possible, two seem of particular significance to us. The author analyzes Konyak society "vertically" in terms of villages, wards, clans, and households, and "horizontally" in terms of three ranks of prestige. Within this framework he describes, in the varying contexts of its functions, the "morung," the bachelor's house. The concept applies not only to the house itself, an imposing structure in which men and initiated boys spend much of their time, but also to the ward of the village of which a specific morung structure was always a social and political focal point. The functions of the morung in its broad sense, and the obligations of identification with it, are most important to an understanding of Konyak sociopolitical organization. Broadly similar groupings, with similar functions, are found in many nonliterate societies over a widespread geographic area. The student of anthropology will find the study of this institution of particular significance.

Another focus that seems especially noteworthy to us is the description of courtship and of premarital, marital, and extramarital sexual behavior. By Western moral standards the Konyak are sexually free. Neither chastity nor virginity is valued. Under certain conditions marital bonds are flexible. Nevertheless marriage has very important social and economic consequences. The economic obligations between affines are widely ramified. Marriages are contracted between families, although under certain conditions the contracts can be nullified. Sexual behavior before marriage and outside of wedlock is governed by group membership and by standards of propriety that are applied to very different aspects of behavior than those customary in Western culture. The author demonstrates very clearly how sexual behavior is culturally patterned, limited, and restricted in a situation where, seen through Western eyes, sexual freedom seems to prevail. Understanding these balances between freedom and restraint is of great importance for the student of anthropology, since some form of them is an integral part of all human cultures.

Other focuses that the reader will find expanded in this case study include: the ecological relationship and social consequences of slash-and-burn cultivation; the daily round of life; political controls and leadership; material culture; and religious rites, including rites of head-hunting. The reader, we believe, will be instructed and intrigued by this case study.

GEORGE AND LOUISE SPINDLER
General Editors

Phlox, Wisconsin
October 1968

Acknowledgments

Most of the information embodied in this account of the Konyak Nagas was gathered in 1936 and 1937, when a research fellowship from the Rockefeller Foundation enabled me to spend thirteen months in the hills on India's eastern frontier. My indebtedness to the Rockefeller Foundation is equaled only by my gratitude to the late J. P. Mills, then deputy commissioner of the Naga Hills district and author of several books on the Nagas; his support and encouragement were of inestimable value during my time among the Konyaks.

I am grateful also to the government of India and the authorities of the North East Frontier Agency for the facilities afforded to me during a visit to the Tirap district in 1962. At a time when few outsiders were permitted to enter any part of the North East Frontier Agency my wife and I were given the most generous help in our travels and anthropological inquiries. We are particularly grateful to Sonu Lovraj, then political officer in charge of Tirap, for his hospitality and spontaneous assistance, and L. R. N. Srivastava, who accompanied us to the Wanchu area and gave us the benefit of his familiarity with the local tribesmen.

To the National Science Foundation and the Wenner-Gren Foundation for Anthropological Research I am greatly indebted for financing this second visit to the Naga country.

CHRISTOPH VON FÜRER-HAIMENDORF

Contents

THE KONYAK NAGAS

An Indian Frontier Tribe

Introduction

THE YEARS FOLLOWING the second world war witnessed a major change in the orientation of anthropological research. Until then anthropologists had been concerned mainly with the study of primitive and preliterate societies, but now they turned their attention increasingly to the peoples of more advanced and complex civilizations. Instead of living with small isolated groups in remote jungles, deserts, or hill regions, anthropologists settled in the crowded villages of India, Mexico, or the Near East, and shared the life of peasants rooted in the traditions of some of the great historic civilizations. In these years it became unfashionable to concentrate on the study of primitive tribes, and many of the younger anthropologists of our day have never had the experience of living in a society which lacks contacts with the modern world.

The time when research among isolated primitive groups is still possible rapidly draws to its close, and it is a sobering thought that in the entire history of the world there are at the most fifty years when the existence of primitive populations more or less unchanged by contacts with technologically advanced civilizations coincides with the availability of apparatus capable of recording with accuracy the style of life of archaic man. Until a few decades ago anthropologists did not have the mechanical means to produce visual and auditory records of a permanent nature, and within some twenty or thirty years when the machine age will have penetrated to the last corners of the world, the objects of such documentation will no longer be in existence. No exertions on the part of future anthropologists will be able to make up for lost opportunities. To them the present preliterate societies will appear as remote and inaccessible as the society of paleolithic man is to us. For this reason I feel justified in presenting here the results of fieldwork among an Indian tribe undertaken more than thirty years ago.

When in 1936 I embarked upon the study of the Konyak Nagas on India's northeast frontier, the interests of most anthropologists were still focused on pre-literate and comparatively isolated societies, and I consider myself fortunate to have had the opportunity of recording an ancient cultural pattern and way of

1

life which was to be disrupted and transformed much sooner than I or anyone else could then have foreseen. Today the society of the Konyak Nagas no longer exists in its traditional form, and the turbulent political situation in Nagaland—one of India's foremost trouble spots—has barred the area to scholars ever since India attained independence. A lucky chance allowed me to visit an adjoining area, the Tirap district in 1962, and there, only some 20 miles north of my previous field of study, I was able to collect data complementary to the results of my earlier research. Though officially described as Wanchu, the people of that area are closely allied to the Konyak Nagas of the present Nagaland, and their inclusion within a different administrative unit is a matter of historic accident. It was accidental too that during the British period their villages had remained outside the administered region then known as the Naga Hills district. After some early brushes with British expeditions the Wanchus had been left to their own devices, and not until after 1947 did the government of India take effective steps to bring them under its administrative control. The middle-aged and older people I met in 1962 had thus spent the greater part of their lives under a political system organized on traditional lines. Here conditions were not very different from those prevailing among the Konyaks of the Naga Hills district a quarter of a century earlier, but the construction of motorable roads and the introduction of school education and medical services were just beginning to make their impact.

The impossibility of ascertaining the extent of recent changes in the cultural life and social system of the Konyaks comprised within the political unit now known as Nagaland has made it advisable to write this entire account of traditional Naga life in the past tense. The decision to use a historic form of representation does not imply, however, that *all* aspects of tribal life have drastically changed, and even less that the Konyaks and Wanchus have undergone a process of social and cultural disintegration comparable to the fate of Australian or American Indian populations. They remain compact and vigorous communities, undisturbed in the possession of their ancestral lands, but their subjection to an outside authority, and the establishment of contacts with populations of different cultural background must inevitably have led to modifications of the traditional social order. To ignore these modifications and use the present tense for a description of a state of affairs observed some thirty years ago would create the misleading impression that life in the Naga hills still corresponds to the picture painted in my earlier book *The Naked Nagas* (1939).

This picture has now paled, but for anthropology it remains significant as an example of an archaic culture of great wealth and complexity. Though adjoining a region which had been dominated by Hindu civilization for several centuries, the Naga hills remained outside the Hindu cultural sphere. Racially as well as culturally the Nagas have close affinities with the hill tribes of the eastern Himalayas (for example, Daflas, Apa Tanis, and Abors), and in some respects they resemble even such distant ethnic groups as the Ifugaos and Igorots of Northern Luzon and the Dayaks of Borneo. All these hill people are characterized by an agricultural economy which, despite considerable efficiency in the cultivation of rice and other grain crops, has never utilized the principle of animal traction and, hence, remained distinct from the peasant economy of the historic civilizations of Southeast Asia. Nagas, no less than most of the preliterate hill people of that part of the world, never knew a source of energy other than human labor, and this limitation implied that virtually the entire population was engaged in the task of tilling the land. Animals were raised for the sole purpose of slaughter; the milking of cattle was as unknown as using them for traction.

The economy of these Southeast Asian hill tribes was thus basically similar to that of the neolithic age, nothwithstanding the fact that even the most primitive among them knew the use of metal, and some were experienced in the working of iron as well as of brass.

In comparison with many of the aboriginal tribes of peninsular India the Nagas stand out by their substantial villages and their rich material culture. Large, well-built houses, often decorated with elaborate carvings, also set them apart from most of the tribes of the Himalayan foothills north of the Brahmaputra, and this efflorescence of technical skills and artistic expression occurred in a habitat inherently not more favorable than the natural environment of tribes much poorer in material possessions.

While most of the aboriginal tribes of peninsular India have to some extent been influenced by Hindu ideas and attitudes, the Nagas and many hill tribes on the northeast frontier have remained outside the sphere of Hindu ideology. Neither in ritual practices nor in the pantheon of divinities and spirits can we detect any affinities to Hindu concepts. This complete separateness in religious matters is quite remarkable, for a limited barter trade between some of the hill people and the Hindu peasantry of the plains of Assam must have gone on for many generations.

The earliest accounts by Europeans on the Naga tribes date back to the first half of the nineteenth century. They are confined to a few superficial descriptions, most of which emphasize the savage character of the Nagas. Thus John McCosh wrote in 1837: "They are the wildest and most barbarous of hill tribes, and looked upon with dread and horror by the neighbours of the plains who consider them as ruthless robbers and murderers" (McCosh, p. 136). Several decades passed before British officials and army officers became more closely acquainted with the Nagas and discovered that they were divided into several distinct tribes. The first ethnographically significant writings on the Nagas were those of S. E. Peal, who toured the Naga hills extensively and between 1872 and 1897 published no less than twelve articles on the Nagas in the *Journal of the Royal Anthropological Institute*. Further early reports on the Nagas are those of R. G. Woodthorpe, J. Butler, and E. W. Clark, an American missionary. In the first decade of the twentieth century there followed articles by L. M. Waddell, W. H. Furness and P. M. Molz, and in 1911 T. C. Hodson published the first monograph on a group of Naga tribes entitled *The Naga Tribes of Manipur*. Three years later J. H. Hutton, for many years senior administrative officer in the Naga Hills district and later professor of anthropology in the University of Cambridge, began his long series of publications on the Naga tribes. His two monographs *The Angami Nagas* (1921) and *The Sema Nagas* (1921) remain anthropological classics, and Hutton was undoubtedly the greatest expert on the Nagas. It is fortunate that his successor as district commissioner of the Naga hills, the late

J. P. Mills, shared Hutton's anthropological interest in the Nagas. His three monographs *The Lhota Nagas* (1922), *The Ao Nagas* (1926), and *The Rengma Nagas* (1937) complete the massive contributions which British officials made to our ethnographic knowledge of the Naga region.

When I arrived in the Naga hills in 1936, J. P. Mills was still in charge of the Naga Hills district, and it was my good fortune to join him on two tours, one through the country of the eastern Angami Nagas, and the second through the then unadministered tribal country close to the Burmese border inhabited by the hitherto virtually unknown Sangtam, Chang, and Kalyo Kengyu Nagas.

The tribe I chose for intensive fieldwork, however, was the Konyak Nagas, and for close to a year I concentrated on the study of this people. The group of villages in which I settled had then fairly recently been brought under British administration, but a much greater number of Konyak villages had remained unadministered, and it was not until 1962 that I had an opportunity to visit some of the previously independent villages.

The following account is based mainly on my research in 1936 and 1937, but some of the information obtained in the area visited in 1962 throws additional light on aspects of Naga society only partially explored in my earlier book. Though Konyak society is rapidly changing, the villages in the Tirap district of the North East Frontier Agency still offer a fruitful field of research, and in this particular part of India it is not yet too late to increase our knowledge of some of the most archaic societies of the Asian continent.

In my approach to the analysis of Konyak society I largely followed the fieldwork methods developed by Bronislaw Malinowski, though my earlier training in Vienna gave me a greater interest in comparative studies than was at that time current among British social anthropologists. For my field of study I chose the large village of Wakching and I lived there with some interruptions from July 1936 until June 1937. Only after I had gained a reasonable understanding of the internal organization of this village did I visit neighboring settlements as well as more distant Konyak villages differing from Wakching in language, political structure, and some aspects of material culture. Wakching, however, remained the focus of my investigation of Konyak society, and only in Wakching did I have close relations with a large number of prominent villagers and a nodding acquaintance with every man, woman, and child. Communication presented a considerable problem. The Konyak dialect is a Tibeto-Burman tonal language of which not even a simple word list was known. Though I managed to compile a vocabulary, a skeleton grammar, and a large number of texts, my knowledge of the language was much too limited for serious conversation. Fortunately, many people, including even some children, spoke fluent Naga-Assamese, the lingua franca of the entire Naga Hills region. Having arrived with a slight knowledge of Assamese, I soon learned to speak and understand this language, and while at first I used an English-speaking Naga youth from another tribe as interpreter, I finally worked entirely through the medium of Naga-Assamese. Fluency in this language enabled me to converse at ease with most men of Wakching, but in other villages where less Assamese was spoken I often had to employ interpreters capable of translating from the local dialects into Naga-

Assamese. There are numerous different and mutually not understandable dialects, and this great linguistic diversity is a characteristic feature of the Konyaks and one which distinguishes them from many linguistically more homogeneous Naga tribes. To ignore this diversity which coincides with a considerable cultural diversity and to concentrate in my work entirely on one village or one linguistic group would have resulted in a one-sided and incomplete picture, whereas the comparison of the divergent culture patterns prevailing in a wider area brought out the wide range of variations within the Konyak social system.

The name Konyak, applied by British administrators to a large and by no means homogeneous ethnic group, is derived from the word *keniak*, which in the language of a small number of villages means "man." It was first heard in the village of Tamlu, which together with the whole tract of country west of the Dikhu River was taken under British administration as early as 1889.

The Konyaks of all villages had traditions regarding the origin and migrations of their forefathers, and many of these myths refer also to the circumstances of the foundation of their villages. Some of these mythical accounts are contradictory, but several main motives occur in the traditions of many villages.

According to one tradition, the ancestors of the majority of Konyaks came from a mountain called Yengyudang situated to the south of the present Konyak territory. Another and equally widespread tradition tells of a migration from the Brahmaputra valley along the Dikhu River and into the hills flanking that river. The tradition of the people of Wakching was more specific. They believed that their forefathers came from a mountain beyond the Brahmaputra known as "mountain beyond the great water." On their way from there they crossed the Brahmaputra valley and followed the Dikhu as far as the present village of Chongwe. Finding that the land there was not sufficiently fertile, they and the ancestors of the people of Wanching migrated to the ridge on which nowadays the villages of Wakching and Wanching are situated, but these early migrants were believed to have been only part of a tribe the other half of which had remained in the hills beyond the Brahmaputra.

Parallel with this tradition of .a migration from a distant land exists a myth according to which most clans of Wakching came out of an immense bird, called Yang-wem-ou-niu, who lives in the water of the Dikhu. Another myth relates how all men and beasts emerged from an enormous gourd, whereupon Gawang, the sky god, divided the earth among them.

While these two latter myths refer to the age when humanity first established itself on earth, the migration myths reflect presumably population movements which led to the present distribution of the Konyaks. The men of Wakching were conscious of the contradictions in these migration myths and explained them by pointing out that not all the clans of the village had the same origin. While the majority of the clans was believed to have crossed the plains of Assam, others were said to have immigrated from the vicinity of Yengyudang and Chongwe. However permanent Konyak villages appear to be now, the myths certainly suggest a time when the country was less densely populated and migrating groups could still carve out new domains for themselves.

Nagas, like many other primitive people, believed that the dead returned to the original homeland, whence their mythical ancestors had come. According to the beliefs of the Wakching men, the departed traveled to the land of the dead by way of the villages of Chingtang, Chinglong, and Chongwe, and the southern direction of this route suggests that at least some elements among the Thenkoh group may have had old associations with that southern region through which the dead were supposed to travel on their way to the nether world.

1

The Material Background

Environment

THE HABITAT OF THE KONYAK NAGAS extends between 26 and 27 degrees north latitude, and thus lies outside the tropics. The climate, however, is basically tropical, though seasonal variations are great. In the summer, temperatures in the valleys rise well above 100° F, and even on the hills, where the villages lie, temperatures in the middle eighties are common. In the winter, however, temperatures in the higher villages may sink at night to below freezing point, and cause acute discomfort to the scantily clad Konyaks. Yet, the more elevated village sites are considered desirable, perhaps because they lie above the malarial zone and are thus healthier than the villages of the foothills.

The rainfall is heavy in the whole of the Naga hills, and at Wakching it amounts to an average of 160 inches per year, the greater part falling between April and September. Narrow valleys, cutting deeply into the hills, are filled with dense evergreen forest. Enormous trees, untouched by fire or axe, rise from the tangled undergrowth, and a thorny kind of cane forms thickets virtually impenetrable if no path has been cleared.

There are no settlements in the dense, virgin forest of the low valleys, and the way from the river beds to any of the Konyak villages leads for about an hour through high tropical rain forest and patches of bamboo jungle. Gradually this forest recedes and gives way to hill slopes covered with bush or low secondary jungle, which is periodically cleared for cultivation. Even when one reaches the fields of rice and taro, the village may still be far away, and before one approaches it, the path leads once more through high shady forest. This is the wood reserve of the village, which provides fuel and timber and may, therefore, never be cleared for cultivation. Such forest, covering the ridges above an altitude of 4000 feet, is largely deciduous and in the spring many trees cover themselves with magnificent white, pink, and red blossoms.

Interspersed with such forest reserves are carefully planted groves of a

Houses in the village of Wanching; in the background the ridge of Wakching.

palm (*Livistona jenkinsiana*) the leaves of which are used as thatch, as well as patches of bamboo which provide the Konyak with material for building and basketwork.

Wakching, the village I studied in 1936 and 1937, occupied the highest point of a broad and somewhat uneven ridge which rose to an altitude of about 4300 feet. With 249 houses, and a population of about 1300 inhabitants, it was the largest village within a radius of about 10 miles. Its size as well as its splendid strategic position had secured it against the attacks of hostile neighbors long before the establishment of Pax Britannica had put an end to head-hunting raids within the Naga Hills district.

To the west and northwest the people of Wakching looked over country long pacified by the British Administration. In this direction lay the foothills, covered by dense tropical rain forest and the broad plains of the Brahmaputra valley, the home of peaceful Hindu peasants and the site of many flourishing tea estates. Beyond this valley one saw on clear days the snowy peaks of the Himalayas, but the Nagas had no conception of the true nature of those dazzling peaks, the nature of snow lying outside the realm of their experience. The plains of Assam, however, held no mystery for the men of the mountains. Their forefathers had been accustomed to raid the low country in search of loot and head trophies, but with the coming of British rule conditions had changed, and now the Nagas descended into the plains for the purpose of bartering their produce against salt, iron, and various manufactured goods.

Eastward and southward of Wakching, a vast tangle of hills extended as far as the Burmese border. But while the villagers' eyes could range over this wide expanse of wooded mountains and cultivated hill slopes, the area within which they could safely travel was strictly limited. Even old men had never entered some of the villages clearly visible on distant ridges, for so precarious was personal security in Naga society that no one dared travel to places where he had neither friends nor kinsmen. Only in the neighboring villages of Wanching and Chingtang did the Wakching people feel entirely at home. Here they were among friends, speaking the same language, wearing similar dress and ornaments, and living in houses of exactly the same type. While Wakching and Wanching were of approximately equal size and politically independent of each other, Chingtang, situated on a lower ridge, was a much smaller village and tributary to both of its more powerful neighbors.

An hour's walk in another direction brought a Wakching man to the small village of Shiong. Here he found himself among people speaking a different language, and dressed and tattooed in a style other than that of his own village.

Turning from Shiong to the northeast he reached, after another hour's walk, the village of Tanhai. The dress of the people of that village resembled his own, but the language differed from the dialects of both Wakching and Shiong. At a distance of less than 3 miles from Tanhai lay the village of Longkhai. Here the visitor from Wakching found himself among a people who spoke yet another dialect, although they dressed in the same way as the Shiong people. He, who was used to living in his own village as an equal among equals, found in Longkhai a chief of aristocratic blood, dominating the community as its undisputed ruler. There, houses were built in a style considerably different from that of Wakching, Shiong, and Tanhai.

In the Konyak country it was thus possible to transverse in a single day several linguistic areas, and the material culture too differed noticeably from village to village. Among most of the other Naga tribes there was much less linguistic and cultural diversity, and in Ao or Angami country one could travel for several days without encountering significant local variations.

The bisection of the Konyak tribe into two groups distinguished by cultural and linguistic features was first recognized by J. H. Hutton and J. P. Mills. They described the two sections of the tribe as Thenkoh and Thendu, expressions which, like the word *keniak*, occur in the language of Tamlu and Tanhai, and refer to the most conspicuous feature of the Thendu men, namely, their elaborate face tattoo, and the absence of such facial decoration among the Thenkoh people. The equivalent names in the language of Wakching are Sheangtu and Sheangshong, but in order to avoid confusion, the names introduced by Hutton and Mills will be retained throughout this book.

The villages of the Thenkoh group occupy part of the outer ranges adjoining the plains of Assam, and in 1937 most of them lay within the borders of the Naga Hills district. They included Wakching, Wanching, Chingtang, Kongan, Namsang, Tamlu, Kanching, and Anaki, whereas the Thenkoh villages Kamahu, Yungya, and Tangsa still lay in unadministered territory.

The Thendu group greatly surpassed the Thenkoh group in size and extension. Within the Naga Hills district the villages of Chingphoi, Shiong, Longkhai, Lungnyu, Hungphoi, Wangla, Oting, Lunglam, and Lapha belonged to this group, but their main strength lay in the unadministered tribal country to the northeast. The Wanchu villages now included in the Tirap district are closely allied to the Thendu group.

A third group, extending to the south and southeast of Wakching and centered on the village of Chen was virtually unknown in 1937, and since no information has since become available it will be disregarded in these pages.

Appearance, Dress, and Ornament

Of all the peoples I have studied the Konyaks were in many ways the physically most attractive. Men and women were of slender build and delicate bone structure, and retained even in middle age their youthful figures and graceful movements. Their facial features were of paleomongolid type, the pigmentation light to medium brown with a ruddy tinge and the eyes dark brown or black.

Both men and women took a great deal of trouble over their appearance, and sported numerous colorful ornaments. Young men and girls were particularly well groomed, their bronze skins clean and their black hair well combed, often with a fresh flower stuck in earlobe or hair knot.

Left: Young man of Longkhai with the tattoo of a head-hunter.
Right: Young girl of Wakching, wearing bead necklaces and brass armlets.

Girls of Chingphoi dressed for the spring festival.

Girl of noble rank in festive dress has her hair brushed, Longkhai village.

In the older literature the Konyaks were sometimes referred to as "naked Nagas," and in 1936 this description was still justified. Men and half-grown boys seldom wore more than a tight belt and a small apron, but at that time the custom of covering the private parts was probably of comparatively recent introduction. Although the young men of Wakching seldom took off their aprons in public, many middle-aged men worked naked in house and field, and on occasions such as funerals, particular functionaries were in the habit of performing their ritual duties naked. And as late as 1962, even young Wanchu men were to be seen without aprons, gossiping in the village or digging in the fields.

Men's belts were made of several coils of cane or of broad strips of bark, with long ends that hung down over the buttocks like a tail. The apron was a rectangular piece of blue cotton cloth which covered the private parts and was tucked into the belt. Old and middle-aged men wore their aprons plain, but boys and young men favored aprons embroidered in red and yellow wool, which was obtained in the markets of the plains. These embroidered aprons were usually the gifts of girlfriends, who in return received such presents as incised combs or ear ornaments.

There were minor local variations in male dress and ornament. Thendu men preferred cane to bark belts for everyday wear, and they took a special pride in reducing the waist to an amazingly small size by pulling the cane as tight as was endurable. Their aprons were longer and narrower than those worn in Thenkoh villages.

Similar variations were observable in women's fashions. The women and girls of Thenkoh villages wore narrow, oblong pieces of cloth wrapped round the waist, with one corner tucked in over the left hip. These skirts were about 10 inches wide and provided all the cover required by Konyak standards of decency; a woman would never take off her skirt in the presence of men, not even when bathing or fishing. Unmarried girls usually wore plain white or blue skirts, but married women preferred skirts with a pattern of narrow horizontal stripes in red and white.

Different customs and fashions prevailed in Thendu villages. Here, an immature girl wore only a string round the waist and sometimes she would even dispense with the string. Occasionally, girls with developed breasts and pubic hair could be seen walking nude in the village, but adult women put on a narrow skirt, usually not more than 6 inches wide. This skirt just covered the private parts, but women felt no embarrassment if menstrual blood appeared on their thighs. For everyday use women of all classes wore the same type of horizontally striped skirts. The skirts worn on ceremonial occasions, however, varied according to a woman's social status. A girl or woman of pure chiefly blood had the right to wear a red and white striped skirt decorated with embroidery, glass beads, and tassels of dyed goat's hair. Women of minor chiefly clan were entitled to similar skirts, but to no decorative tassels. Commoners, however, wore skirts of a darker color, usually blue, and these lacked any kind of ornamentation. All these skirts were woven of cotton, and patterns varied slightly from village to village.

From December until March it can be very cold in the villages on the higher ridges, and at this time of the year men and women wrapped themselves in cotton or bark-fiber cloths. Unlike most other Naga tribes, the Konyaks attached little significance to the patterns of various types of body cloths. Apart from a richly embroidered cloth with red and white stripes, to which only men of the rank of head-taker were entitled, there was no cloth reserved for persons of specific social status. Not even chiefs donned cloths of distinctive pattern. The cloth most commonly worn in Thenkoh villages was a plain blue cloth of a type current also among Ao Nagas. More expensive were cloths of red and white or red and blue stripes. A cloth sometimes worn by men, but more popular among women, was white, decorated with a few narrow stripes of black and red embroidery.

In the villages of the Thendu group none of the cloths typical of Wakching were locally manufactured, but some men wore cloths purchased from Thenkoh people. Here, very little cotton was used, and most textiles were made from the bark fiber of a small shrub of the *Urticacaea* family. Such cloth, woven from bark fiber, was rougher than the local cotton cloth and was generally left the natural color, a dull off-white.

During the rainy months Thendu women working in the fields protected themselves with cloaks which were made on a palm-leaf lattice frame and padded with shredded palm leaves. When it was not actually raining, the women often tied this type of cloak round the hips as an additional skirt. Apart from these rain cloaks Konyak women of all villages wore rain shields and hats of various types. In Wakching women made rain hats by stiffening a palmyra palm leaf with a crisscross of split bamboo. However, they also had more elaborate oblong shields which consisted of pandanus leaves on a cane frame; these were turned in at both ends and protected neck and back. Men and boys never wore rain shields, but in heavy downpours they sometimes tried to protect themselves with a single palm leaf.

Of a different order from the items of everyday dress was the apparel proper for ceremonial occasions. On feast days the boys and men far outshone the women in the variety and splendor of their attire, graded according to their achievements in the field of head-hunting. While at the time of the annual spring festival all males, from small boys to white-haired grandfathers, wore some sort of headgear, only head-takers were entitled to the more magnificent headdresses. Most common were conical hats plaited of red cane and yellow orchid stalks, crested with red goat's hair and surmounted by a few tail feathers of the great Indian hornbill. Head-takers garnished such hats with flat horns carved from buffalo horn and tassels made of human hair. Boar's tusks, monkey skulls, and hornbill beaks were other favorite embellishments, and there was great scope for ingenuity and individual fantasy.

Boar's tusks and antelope horns figured also among the more spectacular ear ornaments, for all Konyaks had perforated ear lobes and wore earrings and studs of great variety.

Among the most cherished ornaments of head-takers were small carved wooden heads worn on the chest. Some of these were of great artistic merit, but similar heads made of brass were of much cruder form.

Both men and women wore arm rings and neck ornaments of various shapes and materials, and many rich men possessed gauntlets covered with cowries and decorated with small tufts of red goat's hair. Only those who had attained the status of head-taker were entitled to wear gauntlets of plaited cane and cane rings dyed red. Cane leggings were worn by all men and boys in years in which a captured head had been brought into the village. On such occasions men plaited the cane onto each other's legs and there the leggings remained until they decayed and fell off.

The ceremonial dress of Konyak warriors also comprised broad, woven baldrics often covered with brightly colored embroidery, and ceremonial hip baskets decorated with all manner of tassels, bird skins, boar's tusks, carved wooden heads and figures, and—in the case of head-takers—also monkey skulls.

Although most types of ornaments were worn throughout the Konyak country, the manufacture of many popular varieties was confined to certain villages or groups of villages. Encroachments on a village's monopoly were rare, and it would seem that on the whole the Konyaks were content to obtain their ornaments by purchase or barter from the traditional producers.

Thenkoh and Thendu Konyaks shared the use of many ornaments, but in hair style and head ornaments they demonstrated a marked individuality. Thenkoh men cut their hair short, but the men of the Thendu group let it grow and tied it up in a knot at the back of the head. Through this they stuck ornaments of several kinds, the most usual being a broad flat wooden "hairpin," sometimes painted red and decorated with tufts of red goat's hair. Head-takers wore longer, batonlike "pins" carved with representations of human heads.

Women's ornaments were not as varied as those of men, and besides the many types manufactured locally from brass and brass alloy, some of which had been handed down from generation to generation and were consequently valued as prestige symbols, most necklets, necklaces, armbands, earrings, and hair ornaments were fashioned from glass beads imported from the plains of Assam.

Thenkoh women of all classes wore their hair long, and those whose hair was not long enough to satisfy their vanity, added false pigtails wound round a length of bamboo, the joint between their own and the false plait being disguised with ribbons of bast.

Among the Thendu Konyaks a woman's hair style was indicative of her social status. All women, except those of a numerically insignificant "slave" clan, who had their heads close clipped, wore their hair long, but in the villages of the Wanchu group only women of noble birth were entitled to long hair and women of commoner clans, even those married as secondary wives to a chief, had to shave their heads.

Weapons

No Konyak ever left his village unless he was armed; he did not feel "dressed" if he had not at least a *dao* stuck in his belt or a spear in his hand. Even small boys carried miniature spears when they went to work in the fields.

The most important weapon and universal implement was the *dao*, an iron chopping knife, with a broad blade, about 8 inches long, hafted on a wood or bamboo handle; the cutting edge was outward curved and the back almost straight. Although valued as a formidable weapon, the *dao* was not only a "head axe" but also a versatile instrument that could be put to many uses in everyday life. It was employed in felling trees, building houses, splitting bamboo, slaughtering cattle and fowls, as well as in haircutting and numerous other domestic tasks. In war the *dao* was used in hand-to-hand fighting and for the decapitation of an enemy slain in battle.

Dao of obsolete type, used neither as weapons nor as implements, but as currency for such ceremonial payments as bride prices, were to be found in the possession of some wealthy men. Such *dao* had very long blades and were much heavier in the hand than those in current use.

The Konyak's main weapons of attack was the spear. In hunting as well as in war, success depended on the effective deploy of this weapon. The ordinary or fighting spear, as carried by adult men, was about 5 feet long; it had a socketed iron head, either lozenge- or leaf-shaped, and an iron butt.

Harpoons of the retriever type were mainly used for spearing fish. They were made up of a plain wooden shaft and a socketed single-barbed head, which was so loosely attached that it left the shaft when it pierced the fish; the coils of the retriever cord unwound as the prey made off and the floating shaft served to point the position of the catch.

Weirs and poison were also used in fishing, and the stupified fish were easily caught in nets and cane traps.

Hunting birds and monkeys with crossbow and arrow was a favorite pastime of both boys and young men. The crossbow was a potentially powerful weapon, with a stave fashioned from bamboo and a stock made of wood. The string was twisted cane fiber and the arrows were bamboo spikes, feathered with finely cut bamboo spathes. The degree of accuracy obtained by Konyaks when hunting small game was not very great, but in the days of raiding, when cross-bowmen played a vital part in defending their village, skillful marksmanship was probably of greater importance. Already in 1936 some muzzle-loading guns were owned by Konyaks, and the increasing use of firearms naturally led to a decline in the art of archery. Yet, even in 1962 there were still crossbows in the hands of the Wanchus of Tirap.

The only defensive weapon carried by Konyak warriors were shields made either of buffalo hide, or of bamboo matting, stretched over a bamboo frame. The former were used in battle as well as at dances, but those made of bamboo were mainly used as dance shields and very occasionally in tiger hunting.

Besides weapons employed in hunting and intervillage feuds, the Konyaks had clubs fashioned from a flattened section of bamboo, with both edges sharpened into teethlike jags. These were used in intravillage hostility, when the young men of rival men's houses came to blows and the taboo outlawing the use of the weapons of war against covillagers had to be respected. In such villages as Namsang, this type of club was kept in the dormitories of unmarried girls, whose lovers used them to ward off the unwelcome attention of other boys.

While all the weapons described above were mainly functional and of simple shape, those intended for display on ritual and festive occasions were elaborately ornamented with colorful trimmings. *Dao* handles were decorated with tufts of goat's hair, usually in alternating bands of red and black. According to established custom, only head-takers were entitled to carry such *dao*, but at the time of my acquaintance with the Konyaks this rule had been relaxed, and any man or boy who had taken part in the ceremonies following the bringing in of a head was permitted to carry a *dao* tufted with goat's hair. Ceremonial spears, sometimes with two-pronged heads, bore similar decorations of red and black goat's hair, and men who had taken more than one head were allowed to carry spears whose shafts were covered with fine plaiting woven from cane, stained red, and yellow orchid stems.

Tools and Household Implements

Compared to the great variety and the decorative character of ornaments and ceremonial dress and weapons, the Konyaks' household utensils and the implements employed in gaining a living were simple and lacking in embellishment.

Apart from a *dao*, which was an indispensable piece of every Konyak's equipment, many a man owned an axe with a flat iron blade inserted in the split head of a wooden handle; but foreign-made axes of handle-holed type were already in use in some of the villages in the late 1930s. Two iron implements made by Konyak blacksmiths were hoe and reaping knife. The hoe, used in weeding and in digging over soft ground, consisted of a small semicircular hoop of iron set between two pieces of crossed bamboo. It resembled in shape and function the traditional hoe, which was made from a single piece of split bamboo, sharpened along one edge, and bent double so that the two ends crossed. The reaping knife or sickle was about 8–10 inches long, and the serrated edge was curved at the end. The only other agricultural implement was a wooden digging stick with a pointed end and this was employed when planting and digging up taro.

Cooking utensils were few and simple. Taro was peeled and vegetables cut up with small knives, and food that was boiled was stirred with wooden ladles. These ladles were also used for serving food from the earthen cooking pots onto the eating platters. Every household possessed a number of round wooden dishes, from which several members of the family were accustomed to eat; they were of good finish and well-balanced shape and were fashioned by the men of the household. There were also smaller dishes of split and bent bamboo, and guests of a rank either higher or lower than that of their hosts ate from these or from freshly plucked banana leaves.

In most Konyak houses there were numerous vessels and flasks for holding liquids. Many were made of gourd, sometimes strengthened with plaited cane covers, and some were fashioned in basketwork, tightly woven and water-proofed with the sap of the *Ficus* tree. Bamboo culms of all sizes were used for transporting and storing water, and women returning from the village spring transported six or seven culms of water in large conical carrying baskets.

Crafts and Techniques

There was a rigid division of labor between the sexes insofar as domestic crafts were concerned. While in agriculture men and women cooperated in many tasks, no women was ever seen making baskets, carving wood, or working metal, and men took no part in pot-making, spinning, weaving, or dyeing yarn.

Basketry was an important craft, for baskets were required for the transport and storage of most commodities. When a Konyak set out on any enterprise, be it trading, or fishing, or a head-hunting raid, he would carry the appropriate type of basket. Men setting out for work on the fields invariably transported their implements in a basket, carried in the customary manner by means of a strap across the forehead; at harvest time the crop was brought home in large conical baskets, and in the granaries rice was stored in big flat-based, coarsely woven basket bins. Baskets were also the only receptacles for the storage of textiles and valuables, and bamboo mats served as seats and as convenient ground cover for such operations as the drying of rice and vegetables. They also formed an important article of trade, for in the plains of Assam the well-plaited Konyak mats and winnowing fans found a ready market. Moreover, bamboo wattle was used as house walls and as flooring on the open platforms of house and morung.

The raw materials for basket-making were bamboo and various kinds of cane, and the instruments employed were *dao*, knife, and, in fine basketry techniques, a spike of bone or metal. Twill and check patterns were the most frequent for mats and the more closely woven baskets, but the Konyaks were also expert in an open-lattice technique in which a hexagonal design was worked on the weft in three directions. If a basket was needed for immediate use, as, for instance, for the transport of a chicken, a Konyak was able to make a rough receptacle in a surprisingly short time.

There were no professional basket-makers among the Konyaks, but every man was able to produce the baskets and mats required by his own household. Whenever there was a lull in agricultural activities, one would find the men sitting on the verandas of bachelors' halls or dwelling houses engaged in making baskets.

Wood-carving was also exclusively a male activity, and no other Naga tribe was as expert in woodwork as the Konyaks. Their public buildings were decorated with carved figures and high reliefs of great force and vitality, and those who were especially gifted as sculptors developed their art in the service of the men's houses, decorating posts and beams and the huge log gongs with realistic carvings. Men modeled the small wooden heads which were worn as ornaments by head-takers, carved such small objects as tobacco pipes, combs, and hairpins, and made all the wooden utensils which were necessary in everyday life. Even small boys were often to be seen whittling away at a piece of wood, producing crude figures of men and animals.

Though there were no professional wood-carvers among the Konyaks, some artists were famous far beyond the borders of their own village. Nevertheless, it was unusual to employ a wood-carver from another village when a new bachelors' hall or chief's houses was to be built. If a specially skilled artist lived in a tributary village, however, a chief might invite him to execute some of the carvings on the new building.

The instruments used in wood-carving were *dao*, knife, chisel, and hammer. When a large wooden post had to be carved, it was given a rough shape while it lay in the forest. Then it was dragged to the village and left to dry for many months. Only then did the sculptor set to work. Some artists drew the outlines of the planned figures with charcoal, but often a sculptor would begin his work with hammer and chisel, hacking chips from the post, until gradually the figure of man or beast grew out of the wood. When the figures had taken shape, the artist began to use his knife for the finer work of retouching.

The artistic merits of the wood sculptures which were to be seen on Konyak buildings varied according to the talents of the man who had carved them, and the quality of carvings differed from village to village. In general feeling and style they were clearly distinguished from the visual art of such tribes as Angamis and Semas. While Angami paintings and carvings were conventionalized, often stylized representations, the peculiarity of Konyak carvings lay in their great naturalism. Humans and animals appeared in movement and were arranged in groups, which, although following certain traditional lines, left ample scope for the imagination of the artist. Human figures were represented in an upright or squatting posture. Men holding enemies' heads and men with raised *dao* were frequent motifs, but there were also men smoking pipes or picking lice from each other's hair. The primary sexual characteristics were always strongly emphasized. Coitus representations adorned the men's houses in several villages, and copulating couples were portrayed standing, though this was a pose not habitually adopted by Konyaks. A frequent subject with an equally strong sexual note was the loving couple, with arms entwined, in dancing postures. There can be little doubt that such phallic symbolism had the purpose of promoting fertility, and the carvings of women giving birth, or carrying a child in their arms, probably had the same aim.

While the human figure was a frequent subject for the wood-carver's art, animals, particularly wild animals, provided equal inspiration. Tigers, elephants, monkeys, and hornbills constituted favorite motifs, while domestic animals were hardly ever depicted. How little the Konyak artist was restricted by a set of traditional motifs was demonstrated by one carving of soldiers with rifles, which had been executed soon after the Konyaks had had their first experience of Indian troops.

Among the Konyaks there were also excellent metal-workers, who were famous for the high quality of their iron weapons and implements, particularly *dao*, and for their brass ornaments. According to an Ao tradition, the earlier inhabitants of their country were expert blacksmiths, and so it is not unlikely that the art of working metal has been long established in some parts of the Naga country.

While every Konyak knew how to make baskets and most had tried their hand at carving wood, the working of metal was practised by specialist craftsmen.

There were men who worked as blacksmiths or brass founders in addition to cultivating their land, but a skilled blacksmith could earn a good living by the sale of the weapons and ornaments he manufactured, and he would often give up tilling the soil. There were villages in which no man worked metal, but in larger villages such as Wakching there were two or three smithies. No blacksmith could work alone; he needed an assistant to blow the bellows, and this task would be undertaken by his wife, or by one of his sons. The craft of blacksmith was often handed down from father to son, but it was not restricted to any particular clan or family. Unlike the blacksmiths of some other Indian tribal populations, the Konyak blacksmiths did not occupy an exceptional social position.

The small hut serving the blacksmith as a workshop stood near his house. In it was the furnace, worked by bellows of the horizontal, one-piston type. Glowing charcoal was used to heat the earthenware air chamber, and the smith, holding the red-hot metal between tongs, hammered it into shape on an iron anvil and cooled it in a stone trough filled with water.

The Konyaks did not know how to smelt iron ore, and all the iron required for the manufacture of weapons and tools was bought from the markets of the plains of Assam, usually in the form of scrap iron and worn out implements.

The manufacture of iron tools and of brass ornaments was not usually undertaken by the same craftsman, but there were many more blacksmiths than brass founders. In 1936 there was only one brass founder in Wakching, and he was a man who had immigrated from the Thendu village of Chi. He was a specialist in the manufacture of a particular type of brass, toothed armlet, and he sold his products to clients of many villages. While the lighter types of rings and armlets were produced by the hammering of red-hot sheet brass, the manufacture of heavy brass ornaments involved the use of molten metal and an expendable clay mold.

Whereas in many societies the craft of the blacksmith is surrounded by an aura of magic, no special powers were attributed to Konyak metal-workers. Nor did they make use of magic to assure the success of their operations. Other activities which involved an element of chance, such as hunting or raiding, were accompanied by magical practices, but no magical formulas were employed to avert mishaps at the forge.

The crafts so far described were the monopoly of men, and women participated only as occasional assistants. Pottery and the manufacture of textiles belonged, however, exclusively to the domain of women.

Only those who were middle-aged or old engaged in pot-making, and although pots were among the indispensable household goods, not all villages produced their own requirements. The Konyaks were unfamiliar with the potter's wheel and modeled each pot by hand from a single lump of clay. When a rough shape had been obtained, the potter proceeded to the final stage of shaping, firming, and thinning and, using a pebble pressed against the inside wall as a stiffener, tapping the outer surface with a flat wooden baton.

Several pots were modeled at a time. They were allowed to dry out before being taken to a place in the jungle where they were set on a low platform of bamboo and covered with wood, which was then set alight. When the firing was completed, the pots emerged a dark-gray color. During the firing of the pots no stranger was allowed to be present, but old men sometimes helped the potter to collect the necessary wood.

All Konyak pots had rounded bases and did not stand without the support of a plaited bamboo ring. When used for cooking, they rested on the stones of the hearth.

The size of pots varied according to the purpose for which they were intended. Small pots with a diameter of about 4 inches were often taken to the fields for boiling tea, but household cooking pots had a diameter of more than 12 inches. To steam rice, Konyaks made pots with perforated bases, and these were placed on top of larger pots in which water was boiling.

While only a minority of Konyak women worked as potters, all girls learned to spin and weave. The raw materials for the manufacture of textiles were the fibers of a small shrub (*Urticacaea Debregasia velutina*) and cotton.

The utilization of bark fiber in the manufacture of cloth was a peculiarity of Thendu villages, and there can be no doubt that in the Naga hills it constituted the older of the two weaving mediums, for no population capable of growing and spinning cotton would adopt the stiff coarse fiber of the Urticacaea shrub and involve themselves in the laborious and complicated methods of processing. The bark had first to be torn to shreds, teased out, and dried. From this a coarse thread was spun on an ordinary spindle, which was weighted by a stone or hardwood whorl. But the yarn was, in this state, too rough to be used for weaving, and long hours of boiling in water were necessary before it became sufficiently pliable and could be woven into cloth.

Cotton could only be grown by villages which had land lying below an altitude of 3000 feet, for on the higher slopes it did not thrive. It was dried on mats spread out on the house platforms, and seeded with the help of a hand-turned machine consisting of two wooden rollers, which revolved in opposite directions. The principle of this machine was undoubtedly an importation from the plains of Assam, and the women of some interior villages continued to seed cotton with the help of rounded pebbles.

Both bark fiber and cotton yarn were woven on a tension loom of a type known to ethnographers as "Indonesian." This loom was portable and could be set up in any convenient flat space, one end being hung up on a post or fence, the other fastened to the waist of the weaver by means of a broad hide belt.

Bark fiber was utilized in its natural coloring, a dull off-white, but for the manufacture of cotton textiles, yarn was dyed and threads of different color were combined in the warp as well as in the weft. The cloth woven on these looms was never wider than about 20 inches, and several strips had to be sewn together to form a body cloth. Needles of bone were the traditional implement used for this work, but even in the 1930s these had largely been superseded by imported needles of steel.

The dyeing of yarn was also done only by women. Red dye was produced from an infusion of the roots of *Rubia sikkimensis*, in which the yarn was allowed to soak for two or three days. Blue and black dyes were the result of boiling indigo leaves in water, the longer the time of boiling, the deeper the color. The process of dyeing was not permitted to those women still capable of bearing a child, but the Konyaks had no explanation for the exclusion of younger women from the dyeing vats. Both weaving and dyeing were occupations which were undertaken during that part of the year in which women had not much work on the fields, that is in the months falling between the bringing in of the harvest and the beginning of the weeding of the following season's crop.

Villages

The Konyaks built—and, indeed, still build—their villages on ridges or spurs from which the land drops sharply into the surrounding valleys. Strategic considerations were certainly uppermost in the minds of most village founders, but the presence of an adequate water supply was also considered an important factor in determining the site of a new village. It is due to the location of springs that many villages were built on saddles or ledges situated a few hundred feet below the highest point of the ridge.

No two Konyak villages were exactly alike. In some the houses were grouped together in one compact block, and enclosed with a fence or stockade, while in others they were scattered over the site in several clusters, interspersed with vegetable plots and bamboo groves. Where there was not sufficient even space to accommodate all the houses on one continuous site, groups of dwellings stood on different levels, often separated by ravines and broken ground.

The number of houses in a village varied between 50 and 250, and a description of Wakching, with its 249 houses, divided into five wards, will give a general idea of the typical layout of the larger villages of the Thenkoh group.

All the approaches to Wakching entailed a long stiff ascent, and the paths climbing the lower slopes of Wakching land passed through areas under cultivation and stretches occupied by the type of secondary jungle that grows on abandoned hill fields. On an open space at the edge of the cultivable land, yet still far below the village, stood long rows of low huts. These were used for storing the firewood collected during the winter months so that in the summer, when field work was pressing, sufficient wood was available for domestic purposes. Close by in the shadow of high trees, spring water collected in a deep hole; and at the top of a flight of stone steps stood a bamboo platform where, during the agricultural season, the girls rested on their way from the fields, singing songs and flirting with their boyfriends.

A broad belt of forest separated the spring from the village and concealed the houses from all who approached. Here, trees were only felled for building purposes and the forest was, in striking contrast to the shrubby bushland which clothed the lower slopes, tall and well grown. Beyond this belt of forest lay a cemetery where, from the hollows of stone receptacles, bleached skulls grinned at passers-by. Funeral platforms carried the bodies of those recently deceased, and on days following a funeral the stench of rotting flesh often caused even the Konyaks to hold their noses as they hurried past.

The corpse platforms stood usually just outside the village stockade. In administered territory fortifications were no longer necessary, and Wakching had given up maintaining a defensive fence. Several nearby settlements had nominal stockades, but Konyak villagers in unadministered territory continued to be on guard, and they surrounded their villages with wooden palisades, the stakes secured with bamboo and cane lashings and spiked with sharpened bamboo spikes.

To both sides of a flight of stone steps which led up to the village stood granaries, small houses with gabled, thatched roofs, which were built on piles 2–3 feet above the ground. Each comprised a storeroom and an open veranda, and here young lovers seeking privacy often spent the night. The owners of the granaries welcomed such nocturnal visitors for their presence lessened the danger from grain thieves. Besides, there was the belief that copulation in a granary promoted the fertility of the seed stored there. A strong double door fastened with wooden bolts barred the entrance to the storehouse, and here, in a rectangular room, stood large store baskets containing rice and millet.

At the entrance to the village a large banyan tree stretched its branches across the path, and passing under this natural porch one found oneself in a large open space. To one side stood a bachelors' hall (morung) and from this large building a gangway on bamboo poles led to a lookout in the high branches. In the days of head-hunting, sentries posted at this vantage point could observe every movement on the path leading up to the village, and in the fields on the slopes far below.

The open space in front of the morung was lined by a circle of flat stones, and in the center stood a menhir and a large stone seat. Each of the men's houses of Wakching had such a dancing place, but not every dancing place was sur- rounded by a stone circle.

On two sides of the dancing ground there were groups of dwelling houses separated one from another by narrow lanes. The houses all faced the street, but often stood so close together that their roofs almost touched. Where the ground sloped away from the back of a house, it was usual to raise the back of the veranda on high poles and thus gain a level expanse of floor.

The sites nearest the morung were considered the best, for there had stood the houses of the "oldest" families, whose ancestors had taken part in the founding of the village. When the households of a ward increased, newly established families had often to build their houses on lower levels at some distance from the morung. In one of the larger wards of Wakching, for instance, whole streets of small houses were strung out down the hillside, but living on the outskirts of the village reflected adversely on a man's prestige.

The houses of a ward, which might number anything between twenty and eighty, were localized in one part of the village. Yet, the boundaries between the wards were not always visible. In some cases there was a narrow belt of shrubs or a ditch separating two wards, but where the number of houses of adjoining wards had inordinately increased, the space which had traditionally divided them had been fully utilized, with the result that houses of different wards stood side by side. Barring exceptional cases, no house site belonging to one ward could be alienated and occupied by a man of another ward, and sometimes it happened that in one ward of a village there might be a surplus of unused, overgrown land, while in an adjacent ward the houses stood crowded together with many built on very uneven ground.

In Wakching, where the institution of chieftainship was in a state of decay, the house of the chief was no larger than the dwelling house of any commoner, but it still occupied the traditional site on one of the highest points of the village and stood close to the Ang-ban, the chief's morung. In front of it there was a group of small stones, where an important ceremony connected with the bringing in of captured heads used to be performed.

In Thendu villages the chief's house occupied a dominant position both physically and socially, and often, in its enormous size, overshadowed even the bachelors' halls. There were also other differences in the layout of Thendu and Thenkoh villages.

While the settlement pattern of Thenkoh villages resembled in broad outline that which I have described for Wakching, the layout of Thendu villages made no provision for the storage of wood outside the village, nor for the storage of grain in granaries at the entrance gate; the individual villager built up his wood reserves under his own roof and kept his grain in a small granary near his own dwelling house.

Community Houses

Of all the men's houses or bachelors' halls of the Naga tribes, those of the Konyaks were the largest and most imposing and their role in the social life of the village corresponded to their striking appearance. In the dialect of Wakching they were described as *ban*, but here I shall use the more familiar Assamese term "morung," which has attained wide currency in anthropological writings on the hill tribes of northeastern India.

Structurally, the Konyak morungs were of two types: those of open front and long protruding gabled roof, and those of closed front, whose roof hung low over a front porch. Both types occurred in Thenkoh as well as in Thendu villages, and there were villages which contained men's houses of both types. In Wanchu villages I saw only morungs of the second type.

The men's houses of such large Thenkoh villages as Wakching were solidly constructed buildings of immense size. The Thepong morung of Wakching, as I knew it in 1936, was 84 feet long and 36 feet broad. The gabled roof was thickly thatched with palm leaves and at the sides the eaves almost touched the ground. A miscellany of leaf bundles, flat decorated sticks, and small carvings of birds were hung from the front ends of the roof rafters and from the thatch, so that they formed a curtain which gave the open porch protection against the sun. This porch extended across the entire width of the building and was about 24 feet deep. Enormous boards 3–4 feet wide and 2 feet high, hollowed on the underside, were set up on three sides of the porch and provided convenient benches on which to work and sit. It was in this porch that most of morung activities took place. In the morning the boys and men who had slept in the morung warmed themselves at the fires burning on two hearths, and later in the day men used the

A Bachelors' hall (morung) in Wakching at the time of the head-hunting rite.

Interior of morung in Wakching with carvings of an elephant and men.

porch as a convenient place in which to make baskets, repair mats, and do all manner of odd jobs while they gossiped with their morung friends. On feast days men assembled on the porch and drank rice beer and tea, and on certain occasions they were joined by their wives, sisters, and daughters. For unlike the men's houses of the Ao Nagas, those of the Konyaks were not closed to women, and when men of a neighboring village came visiting, the girls of the Wakching morung danced with them in the central hall. On ordinary days, however, women did not enter the men's house.

Three large posts, the central one as much as 3 feet in diameter, supported the front of the roof and a corresponding number were ranged along the back of the porch. The style of the carvings decorating such posts has already been described, but not all morungs were entitled to all types of carvings. In Wakching, the Thepong morung contained figures of tigers, but not those of men or elephants, whereas the Oukheang morung was decorated with representations of elephants, but lacked representations of men and tigers. The three remaining morungs, known as Ang-ban, Balang, and Bala were, however, permitted carvings of both men and elephants, but no tiger appeared among the motifs adorning their posts.

In some morungs the carvings were painted with bright color washes, but to have painted carvings was a privilege to which not all morungs were entitled. Thus, in Wakching only one morung contained painted carvings, whereas in the three morungs of Wanching all carvings, the posts and benches of the porch, and the log gong were painted in red, black, and white.

The open porch doorways led into the central hall, which in the case of the Thepong morung was 33 feet long. The floor was covered by stamping boards, which resounded under the feet of dancers at nocturnal feasts. To both sides of the hall lay the sleeping compartments, partitioned off with bamboo matting. In most morungs these small rooms, which contained a number of bamboo bunks, were pitch dark. There was no regulation of roommates for either clan or age-group members, but usually boys of the same age occupied the same compartment.

A door at the back of the hall led into a gallery, and beyond, an open platform built on poles stretched out over the hill slope. This platform served as a useful vantage point from which to defend the village path, for warriors stationed there could shower spears and arrows on an approaching foe without themselves being exposed to the arms of the raiders.

The men's houses of most Thendu villages lacked the open front porch so characteristic a feature among the Thenkoh, and from the outside were indistinguishable from large dwelling houses. One of the morungs was usually called the *Ang*-morung and stood opposite the chief's house. Here was kept the majority of captured heads, and in the hall stood a large wooden chief's seat, decorated with carvings of hornbill heads.

Many morungs were so well constructed that the main posts lasted for more than a generation, but roof and walls had to be replaced every five years; in Wakching it was customary to rebuild a morung about once in twenty years.

Like the Aos and other Nagas, the Konyaks possessed large wooden gongs or xylophones, often inaccurately described as log drums, which stood either in special gong houses, or in the front porch of a morung. About 25 feet in length, such a log gong was hollowed from the bole of a single tree. It had a slit running through almost the whole length of the upper side and both ends were shaped in the form of a canoe's prow; this "prow" was decorated with carvings of geometric design and motifs such as suns and human figures. During head-hunting rites baskets containing captured heads were hung up on the gong and two lines of drummers, standing on boards to either side, beat out the appropriate rhythm with wooden mallets.

The carving and dragging in of a new gong was a great event in the life of a Konyak village and one that was even rarer than the rebuilding of a morung. Unless a gong perished by fire, it would last for many decades, and not every generation of morung members had the opportunity of participating in the elaborate ritual accompanying the manufacture of a new instrument.

The tree chosen for a gong was ceremonially felled with the cooperation of members of another morung, who render their services on a reciprocal basis. After the gong had been roughly shaped in the forest, a process which was accompanied by the sacrifice of a pig, all the people of the morung and ward for which the gong was intended dressed themselves in ceremonial attire and gathered round the half-finished gong.

With the help of cane ropes and wooden rollers they hauled the gong to the village, chanting as they dragged it up the hill. The girls of those morungs which provided ceremonial partners as well as spouses for the owners of the new gong were expected to lend their assistance. When the gong reached the village,. a great feast was celebrated, and the wives, sisters, daughters, and also the potential mates of the host morung joined in the eating and drinking.

The following day, the best craftsmen in the morung began to work on the carving and ornamentation of the gong. On the fifth day after the elapse of one lunar month, the gong was dragged to the place where it was to be housed, either in a gong house or in the porch of the morung. Again a pig was sacrificed and prayers were intoned for the long life of the men of the morung. Where headhunting persisted, it was customary for the men of the morung to capture a human head at the time of the installation of a log gong, and it was laid on top of the new instrument. In Wakching and other administered villages raiding was replaced by a hunting expedition, and the leg of an animal slain in the chase served as a substitute for a head trophy.

A gong was beaten on various ceremonial occasions. There was no "drum language" of the African type, but specific rhythms served to announce a limited number of events: the death of a chief, the capture of a head, and the celebration of certain rituals. Usually the gong was beaten by a company of twelve to sixteen, with a leader who wielded two heavy wooden pestles, two soloists using one pestle each, and the rest of the players, each using one pestle, hitting the wooden gong in unison.

Usually, a gong was played by the men and boys of the morung to whom it belonged, but there were occasions when men of a neighboring village, who were paying a ceremonial visit, played their hosts' gong to honor, for instance, a deceased chief. During the initiation rites held for the boys entering a morung or during the celebrations following the bringing in of an enemy's head, it was appropriate for the girls and women of the morung to beat the gong.

The girls' dormitories, known in the Wakching dialect as *yo*, corresponded to the morung in the sense that every ward of a Thenkoh village had such a dormitory for the young unmarried girls. Unlike the bachelors' halls, however, these dormitories were inconspicuous buildings and had no ritual significance for the community. They were built, not by the men of the girls' own ward, but by the boys and unmarried young men of the morung, which furnished traditionally the partners and mates of the girls who occupied the *yo*.

While such a *yo* served as a club for all the girls of a ward, there was often not enough room to accommodate all of them for the whole night. Some girls slept, therefore, in groups of three and four in the houses of people who had enough space to set apart a small room as an improvised girls' dormitory.

Houses

No one could fail to be impressed by the spaciousness and stateliness of the average Konyak house. It compared favorably with the homes of many Assamese peasants, and offered more comfort than the dwellings in which the majority of the poorer classes of Indian towns were accustomed to live. Differences between the houses of the rich and those of inpecunious families related to size and maintenance rather than to structure and style. There were none of the visible and demonstrative symbols of wealth so characteristic of such Naga tribes as the Angamis, whose affluent men gained the right to decorate their houses with conspicuous carvings by giving costly feasts of merit.

The type of house prevalent in most villages of the Thenkoh group can best be illustrated by describing the house of a moderately wealthy man of Wakching, Yongang, one of the leading figures of the Thepong morung.

Yongang's house stood in a street which led from the Thepong morung to the center of the village. The street was about 12–15 feet wide, and the houses on either side were built so close together that their eaves almost touched.

The front of the house was roughly semicircular, and in its center lay the entrance, some 4 feet wide. Stepping over a low bamboo barrier, placed in the doorway to keep out stray animals, one found oneself in a porch some 16 feet broad and 7 feet deep. The left corner was partitioned off as a pigsty, and to the right a stout wooden door opened into a corridorlike hall, which occupied one side of the entire length of the house. It was some 33 feet long and about 6 feet wide, and here stood a rice-pounding table, 10 feet long, which had been carved from a single block of wood. Half-way down this hall, a large opening gave access to the living room. This was the room in which the family lived, where all meals were cooked and eaten, where guests were entertained, and where the women did most of the housework. In the center was the hearth of three stones and about 3 feet above it a plaited-bamboo, two-tiered tray hung from the roof rafters. The bottom shelf was used for drying rice, and the top shelf for storing foodstuff out of reach of the rats. The floor of this room, which was of pounded earth, was partly covered with bamboo mats.

Close to the hearth stood a small stool for the use of the householder, and there were bamboo bunks standing against the walls. One of these Yongang shared with two of his children, while his wife slept with two other children on a bed at the opposite end of the room.

Baskets, fishing nets, and agricultural implements were hung up on the

A newly built house in Wakching being thatched with palm leaves.

walls and suspended from the roof. Spears stood in one corner and *dao* were stuck in the matting walls. Utensils used in the preparation of food, cooking pots, pounding pestles, wooden ladles, and dishes were grouped within reach of the hearth. All belongings not in frequent use were packed up in closely woven cane baskets and securely closed with lids. Such baskets, used as receptacles for textiles and ornaments, were safe from the depredations of rats and were more or less waterproof.

There was no outlet for the smoke, and the only source of light was a small door in the outer wall of the living room which opened on to the narrow lane separating Yongang's house from that of his neighbor.

At the back of the house the hall widened into a spacious utility room, which stretched across the whole width of the house. This was the stage for such activities as the spreading out and drying of rice and taro,[1] the dismembering and cutting up of animals slain for food, and for the entertainment of guests too numerous to be accommodated in the living room. Here stood the baskets used in the preparation of rice beer, and it was in this room that confinements took place.

The back door of the house led on to a veranda erected on bamboo piles above the slope of the hill. The veranda measured 15 by 20 feet, and about one-third of it was protected from sun and rain by the protruding roof of the house. A railing surrounding the veranda provided convenient support for the drying of clothes. To one side there was a latrine, sheltered from the house by a screen of palm leaves, and the excrement falling to the ground was eaten by pigs roaming among the piles.

---

[1] Taro (*Colocasia antiquorum*) is a root crop widely cultivated in Oceania and Indonesia, but of only minor importance in mainland Asia; its starchy tubers are peeled and boiled in water. Nagas consider taro a food greatly inferior to rice.

In fine weather the family liked to work on this open veranda. Here men made baskets or fashioned and repaired wooden implements, and women spread the mats on which they dried rice and taro, made pots, cleaned raw cotton, and busied themselves with spinning, weaving, and sewing.

The roof of the house rested on three stout mainposts which carried a long ridge pole and a framework of bamboo rafters. It was thickly thatched with layers of palmyra palm and provided excellent protection against the elements.

Structurally, the houses of most Thendu villages were similar to the type described here, but there was some difference in the allocation of the space enclosed within the four walls of the house. The main difference related to the sleeping quarters of unmarried girls. Whereas in Thenkoh villages adult girls were accustomed to spend the night in girls' dormitories, in Thendu villages there were no separate buildings for girls, and most dwellings contained a room where unmarried girls slept and could receive the visits of young men. Usually, the girls of several families congregated in such a room, and in the large houses of chiefs there were girls' rooms similar in function to the girls' dormitories (*yo*) of the Thenkoh villages. The houses of some of the paramount chiefs were of enormous size and contained several large halls for entertainment and gatherings, as well as numerous rooms for the use of the chief's many wives and children. The largest of these chief's houses measured was 360 feet long.

Land Tenure and Agriculture

Most of the tribal populations inhabiting the hills on India's northeast frontier practise a system of soil utilization known as slash-and-burn cultivation. This type of shifting cultivation is well suited to mountainous country of tropical zones where the rainfall is substantial. It cannot support a very dense population, but where land is ample and cultivation can alternate with long periods of fallow, the yield from slash-and-burn cultivation is not necessarily inferior to that attained by more permanent forms of tillage. Shifting cultivation was prevalent among many of the tribal populations of middle and south India, but there, shortage of land and the claims of forest conservancy have in recent years restricted its scope. In countries such as Burma, Thailand, Malaysia, and Laos, as well as in parts of Indonesia, however, most hill people continue to practice this type of agriculture.[2]

In many areas slash-and-burn cultivation on frequently shifted fields is associated with a system of communal ownership of land and often also with a considerable instability of settlements. Ownership may be vested in a territorial group, a village, a clan, or a chief, who, though nominally the proprietor of the entire village land, is under an obligation to distribute it for cultivation to his subjects. Tribes, such as the Aos, the southern neighbors of the Konyak, recognize private as well as communal rights in land, but there are tribes, such as the Daflas in the hills north of the Brahmaputra, who lack the concept of private property in land. They have so little attachment to the soil that settlements are very imper-

[2] J. E. Spencer, *Shifting Cultivation in Southeastern Asia*, University of California Press, Berkeley and Los Angeles, Calif., 1966.

manent, and it is rare for two or three successive generations to remain resident in the same area.

In contrast to such mobility and the consequent fluidity of social units, the Konyaks have for centuries had lasting links with ancestral village sites, and nearly all land was privately owned.

The territory of a village such as Wakching extended over a large area, and comprised virgin forest, cultivable land partly overgrown by secondary jungle, and wasteland unsuitable for economic use. Within that territory all members of the village community were entitled to hunt, irrespective of the rights of individuals to specific cultivable plots. Apart from the arable land which was privately owned, there were also some plots which belonged to particular men's houses, and such morung land was cultivated jointly by the members of the morung.

A man's holdings were never contained in a compact block, but were scattered over the village territory. The richest men of Wakching owned 250 plots, and even men considered poor owned land in several places. The Konyak system of shifting cultivation made such a dispersal of holdings necessary, for every year the village took a clearly defined tract under cultivation and it was desirable that within this tract each family should own land sufficient for its needs. In the following year an adjoining tract was cleared of jungle and cultivated concurrently with that tilled the previous year. The result of this system of rotation was that each field was cultivated over a two-year period, and then lay fallow for several years.

On the whole about one-seventh of the village territory was open for cultivation in any one year, but as even within this area only about half the plots were actually cleared and tilled, it meant that every individual holding was cultivated only once in fourteen years. This was a satisfactory cycle of rotation, for in the intervening period of fallow, secondary jungle covered the land and prevented erosion. By the time the forest was to be felled once more, the land had recuperated and the ashes of the fired jungle provided an adequate fertilizer. There were two reasons for this system of rotation, which assured that all villagers would cultivate on two compact and usually adjoining areas. First, such compact areas cleared of jungle could be guarded more easily than dispersed plots, for individual families and labor gangs could work within sight of each other, and in the days of head-hunting, a small force of young warriors stationed at two or three vantage points could effectively protect all the women and children working on the fields. Second, large areas of cultivated land were less vulnerable to the depredations of birds and animals than individual fields set in the midst of forest. The boundaries between fields of different owners were marked by stones erected at the corners of each plot, and by lines of a flowering plant sown in between the fields. The size of fields was measured by the number of baskets of seed required at sowing time.

Although in Wakching the cycle of rotation was so well established that no one doubted which part of the fallow village territory would next come under cultivation, the decision was made annually in a formal manner. Every autumn, usually in October, those representatives of the five morungs who formed the village council met in the house of the chief and consulted omens by breaking eggs and, from the patterns made by the whites, deduced which slopes the villagers should clear for cultivation in the following year.

Villages differed in the importance they attached to these omens. In Wakching the cycle of rotation was so firmly rooted in accepted practice that the villagers did not seriously allow themselves to be deflected if the omens were bad, but risked a less abundant harvest rather than upset the customary cycle. In Longkhai, however, more attention was paid to the omens: If they were clearly unfavorable, another part of the village land was selected for cultivation. At the same meeting the morung officials admonished the villagers not to damage each other's crops and not to steal from fields or field houses; whoever disobey this order would be fined. Such fines were used for the purchase of pigs to be eaten by the members of the council.

The clearing of the jungle in the area earmarked for cultivation was done by the owners of individual plots. Sometimes the work was done entirely by members of the owner's family, and sometimes kinsmen helped each other on a basis of reciprocity. The older men and women cleared the undergrowth, while the young men felled the trees. A few of the trees were spared, but were so severely pollarded that their shade did not affect the growth of the crop. By allowing such trees to remain standing in the midst of the fields the Konyaks protected their land against erosion and facilitated the regeneration of the jungle at the end of the period of cultivation.

The felled trees and cut undergrowth were left to dry for several weeks and then set on fire. In January smoke rose from many of the hill slopes of the Konyak country, and on windless days a dense gray haze enveloped the landscape. The ashes of the burnt jungle improved the soil, and as the Konyaks did not use any other type of manure, they relied heavily on the fertilizing power of this wood ash.

The burning of the forest did not complete the preparation of the fields. Before sowing could begin, all charred wood had to be collected and disposed of, and the soil cleaned and superficially dug over. At this time the cultivators built field huts in which they could take shelter from rain or the heat of the sun. Considerable importance was attached to the building of these field huts, and before ordinary villagers could begin the work of construction, a village official belonging to a clan associated with the foundation of the village had to ceremoniously build a field hut on his own land. In most villages the chief's field hut was built next, and only then were the other villagers allowed to proceed with the work. The same dignitary who in this way initiated the cultivation season acted also as "first sower" and later as "first reaper," functions to which all Naga tribes attributed great importance.

It is a characteristic feature of Naga society that important operations must be inaugurated by persons of special ritual status; other villagers are not supposed to engage in such activities until a beginning has been made by those destined for the task by descent and status.[3]

---

[3] Cf. C. von Fürer-Haimendorf and J. P. Mills, "The Sacred Founder's Kin among the Eastern Angami Nagas," *Anthropos*, Vol. 31, 1936.

In the middle of January the sowing of the rice was formerly initiated. A man of the lineage of the village founder took the seed of all the six varieties of rice grown by Konyaks and sowed them in a specially prepared small patch of his own field. This ritual first sowing was preceded by the sacrifice of a chicken and a prayer for good crops was addressed to Gawang, the sky god. As he scattered the seed, the "first sower" prayed that the "rice plants might grow well and be unharmed by weeds" and that "the beaks of birds and the mouths of rats and mice should be closed." On the same day the village chief sowed rice on his field, and it was only after these ceremonial sowings had been completed that other villagers could begin to sow their own rice. At that time men and women carrying baskets of seed rice would set out for their fields, with a flowering branch of a peachlike fruit tree stuck in the grain.

The sowing of rice and millet was done exclusively by men, but women working in a line behind the sower, covered the grain with earth. Both rice and millet were broadcast, and the sower usually carried the seed in a large cloth bag slung over his shoulder.

The planting as well as the harvesting of taro was exclusively women's work. Using digging sticks and small *dao*, they dug holes, and in these they planted the tubers. A man would have been ashamed even to carry taro to or from the fields.

Rice was by far the most important and also the most highly valued crop. When its young shoots covered the hill slopes with a dense carpet of luminous green, the villagers enjoyed little leisure, for in between the rice sprouted weeds,

Men of Wakching broadcasting rice while women cover the seed with earth.

and these had to be laboriously eradicated. Each field was weeded several times, and as the cultivated areas were large, men and women spent many weeks working with bent backs in their fields.

To enliven the monotonous task of weeding, boys and girls of different morung joined forces and worked side by side. The boys of one work gang would invite their girlfriends to go with them to the fields, and on the following day they would in return help these girls with the work on the fields of their parents. The girls had to be from a village ward from which the boys could take wives, and the young people working together were, hence, potential mates and often already lovers. Many a romance began in the rice fields at weeding time, and wherever such mixed labor groups were at work, there was much laughing and joking. Toward the end of the weeding the boys of the gang would entertain their girlfriends in one of the field huts, and on that occasion they took pride in providing sufficient rice beer to make their guests drunk. If the girls could not walk unaided the boys would carry them home on their backs and deposit them proudly at the houses of their parents.

A few days later the girls would return the hospitality, and then it was their ambition to make the boys drunk. Two girls might then drag or carry one of their intoxicated friends up the hill to the village.

Cooperation between boys and girls of intermarrying village wards was permitted only at the time of weeding. Neither in the clearing of the fields at sowing time nor during the harvest was the formation of such mixed labor gangs customary.

The rice harvest was inaugurated by a festival lasting for two days during which all work outside the village ceased. At the beginning of the feast a descendant of the village founder went to his fields and cut a few ears of each of the six varieties of rice; these he hung up in his own house. This ceremonial first reaping was followed by the slaughter of cattle and pigs. Kinsmen and families linked by marriage exchanged presents, while the young girls prepared millet breads and distributed them to boys and young men, who moved chanting from one girls' dormitory to the other.

In the old days the warriors often tried to capture a human head for this festival, and if they succeeded there was singing and dancing in ceremonial dress, but since the suppression of head-hunting the harvest festival has been celebrated in a calmer atmosphere. Unlike the harvest festivals of other nations it took place at the beginning and not at the end of the harvest.

On the days following this festival all the villagers went to their fields and began cutting the rice. This was done with small sickles and the men and women of a family worked side by side. The sheaves were carried into the field hut, where a large mat was spread out. On this the men trod out the grain with their feet. The rice was then collected and taken to the granaries on the day it was reaped.

To carry the heavy baskets full of grain up to the village was hard work, and this task fell largely to the women. At this time, as, indeed, throughout the cultivating season, the owners of fields lying comparatively close to the village had to expend much less energy than those whose land lay at a distance of 3 or 4 miles. For this reason, rich men found it useful to rent land close to the village, and perhaps let out any plots of their own which were inconveniently situated. In 1936 the rent for such fields was usually paid in cash, but as money had no place in traditional Konyak economy, there can be no doubt that previously grain was paid as rent for land.

Wealthy people cultivating many fields had also to hire labor in excess of that provided by the members of their own households, and the gangs of unmarried boys or girls who habitually worked together were the most obvious source of such labor. The owner of the field had to feed the members of the gang, and, in addition, pay them a daily wage. This was usually not distributed among the members of the gang, but was kept in a fund used to meet expenditures on feasts. Occasionally, even labor gangs from neighboring villages were employed, and this system of paid labor made it possible for some men to cultivate as many as ten fields in one year. Men who could not afford to hire workers usually contented themselves with the cultivation of two fields. In exceptional cases impoverished men would not cultivate any plots of their own, but worked exclusively for rich people, who paid them partly in rice and partly in cash.

Apart from the cultivation of individually owned fields, there was also some communal utilization of land. A morung, which usually owned only a few strips of jungle, would rent a sizable field and cultivate it through the joint efforts of its members, with the intention of using the yield for the celebration of morung feasts. Not only the young men of the morung but also their sisters would cooperate in tilling such a field.

In villages with powerful chiefs all villagers joined in the cultivation of the chief's land, and even comparatively insignificant chiefs, such as the Ang of Wakching, were given free help with their agricultural work. Such obligations toward chiefs, however, will be discussed in the context of the relations between chiefs and commoners.

Another occasion for cooperation between all the members of a village ward was at the time of harvest, when it was essential that the rice should be transported to the village as speedily as possible. Every morning one man from every house of the quarter would go to the fields of one of their morung fellows and help him with the transport of his grain. Next day a similar team would perform the same task for another member of the ward.

Compared to many of the tribal populations of other parts of India, the Konyaks had an ample and well assured supply of food. Thanks to abundant and reliable rainfall, crop failures were rare, and there was no shortage of cultivable land. The average Konyak family, therefore, never lacked an adequate diet, and only the most improvident and inefficient had ever to fall back on the charity of their kinsmen. Rich people were able to accumulate large stores of grain, and some men of Wakching possessed rice bins filled with a surplus of grain from the harvests of two or three years.

The production of an ample food supply facilitated the growth of villages of a size and stability elsewhere associated only with permanent tillage. Land was the principal source of wealth, and a Konyak had no other effective way of accumulating capital except to increase his holding of land. Pigs, buffaloes, mithan,[4] and ordinary Indian cattle were kept for slaughter, but there was little trade in animals, and none of the systematic investment in livestock which characterizes the economy of more mobile slash-and-burn cultivators such as the Daflas of the Himalayan foothills.

Daily Life in a Konyak Village

The changing seasons involved the Konyaks in a varied rhythm of agricultural activities and numerous festivals and ceremonies which interrupted the routine of farm work, and diverted, often for several days at a time, the villagers' interests from agricultural to social and ritual affairs, but in spite of the diversity of occupations and interests, the Konyaks recognized a prescribed schedule for their daily activities, and the language of a village such as Wakching contained fixed terms for the times of day which were properly devoted to regular activities. In the absence of any other measure of time, these terms allowed the Konyak to identify with adequate precision the times of the day and the night.

Ou-wang-ga-bu, "the time of the first cock's crow," was reckoned as the beginning of the day. The villagers were still asleep: married couples with their small children in their own dwelling houses, older boys and unmarried men in their morung, adult girls in their dormitory, and lovers on the verandas of granaries, situated on the periphery of the village. At *ou-wo-ga-bu,* "the time of the second cock's crow," lovers separated, the girls returning to their dormitories, and the boys to their morung.

Ou-gem-ga-ba, "the time of the third cock's crow," was the time for married women to rise from their beds. They began husking rice or millet for the morning and midday meals and the village reverberated with the dull thud of wooden pestles on wooden pounding tables. As the gray of dawn crept through the village the women winnowed the grain they had pounded, and when the first glimmer of light pointed the housetops against the sky, groups of women set out to fetch water, hurrying down the steep stone steps to the springs located below the village. Little girls accompanied their mothers and even children not more than three or four years old could be seen carrying water home in minute bamboo vessels. After returning from the spring, the women began to prepare the morning meal. The embers of the hearth in the center of the living room were stirred and new wood added to the fire. Rice, taro, or millet were set to boil in earthen cooking pots. This hour was called *shum-bong-bu,* "time before sunrise." While breakfast was cooking, women fed the pigs with taro peelings and a mash made from the previous day's kitchen refuse. Men who were early risers emerged from their blankets, but others slept on until sunrise, the hour known as *wang-he ya-ong.*

This was followed by *nep-ning hei-ya-dzang,* the "time of eating rice." Boys and unmarried men came from the morung and joined their parents and

---

[4] Mithan (*Bos frontalis*) is a type of cattle allegedly related to the wild gaur (*Bos gaurus*) and occurring mainly in the hill regions of northeast India and Burma. Mithan are powerful animals which are rarely fully domesticated and are never used for milking or for traction.

sisters at the family hearth; adults and children squatted round the fire and ate the morning meal, which consisted of rice and whatever spice or relish was available.

Breakfast was a leisurely meal and even when it was finished, Konyak men took their time before embarking on the work of the day. At the time known as *tai-dzim*, "getting together for going," roughly corresponding to 9–10 A.M., the men and boys lounged on the platforms of houses and bachelors' halls, chewing betel, smoking pipes, and gossiping. The time when they set out to work on the fields was called *tai-wing*, "all-go," and men, women, and sometimes children left the village in small household groups or in larger labor gangs, hurrying in single file along the path to the fields. As the Konyaks' system of slash-and-burn cultivation involved the periodic tillage of land extending over a large area, some of the fields under cultivation were likely to be situated at a distance of more than an hour's walk from the village and the sun would stand high in the sky before a man started to work on his fields.

The period of time that followed was named not after any of the tasks connected with agriculture but after a rather inconsequential feature of village life; it was called *ak-sheang-yang-ē*, "pigs' water drying," which referred to the drying remnants of the watery mash fed to pigs in troughs.

During the greater part of the day the village appeared deserted of all but the very old and the very young. Here and there on a veranda an aged man or woman sat in the sun, and children too young to be of use in the fields, played in groups in the village streets and lanes, but to guard against accident or emergency, or in case of fire, several men from each bachelors' hall always remained in the village.

What happened inside a village during the middle hours of an ordinary working day was of comparatively little importance, for each morning during the agricultural period the social life of the village was transferred to the fields, where family worked with family and labor gangs were employed on a basis of cooperation and reciprocity or hired by those sufficiently wealthy to engage them. No Konyak enjoys long periods of sustained work, and even agricultural activities were carried out in a leisurely manner, with periods of digging, sowing, or reaping alternating with times of relaxation, when girls and boys would flirt with each other and married couples retired to a field house and refresh themselves with sips of rice beer or tea.

Noon was called *ni-ning-hei-ha-dzang*, "the time of eating rice," and those working in the fields ate the rice that the women had cooked that morning, either plain or with the addition of some freshly prepared taro and vegetables.

There was no special term to denote the hours of the early afternoon, but the time approximating to 4 P.M. was called *teang-tep-en-ong-dzang*, "time of returning from taro fields," for at this hour those women who had dug up taro growing on fields cultivated the previous season started on their way back to the village.

En-ngui-dzang was the "hour of sunset," and this was soon followed by *en-dzim-bu*, "coming-home time," when men and women and boys and girls stopped work on the fields and returned to the village. The married men and women went home, the women to cook the evening meal, and the men to visit the morung or the house of one of their friends, but boys and girls liked to gather at dusk on the open platforms outside the village. There they gossiped and joked, or sang alternating chants until nightfall, a time called *wang-mang-phong*, "sky dark."

While the evening meal was cooking, many women had to go once more to fetch water from the spring, but for men there was little to do but gossip and smoke with their morung friends.

Not until 8 or 9 P.M. did all the members of a household assemble for the evening meal, which again consisted of rice, taro or millet, and boiled vegetables. This period of time was called *ya-ming-he-ha-dzang*, "time for eating rice in the evening."

Late at night the boys and unmarried men went to the bachelors' hall, and this hour was called *ban-dzim*, "bachelors' hall gathering." Then followed *yo-dzim*, "girls' dormitory gathering," when the boys would collect in the dormitories of their traditional girlfriends and spend the evening in singing and chatting. Then came *yo-weng*, "leaving the girls' dormitory," the hour when boys would either part from the girls of the dormitory and return to their own morung, or go with a lover to one of the granaries, where the couple could spend the night.

Ou-shou, the "time before cock's crow," was that part of the night when the silence of the sleeping village was only disturbed by the occasional barking of dogs.

The daily routine which has been described here applied only to the period of cultivation, a period beginning in December with the clearing of the jungle on the new seasons fields and ending in October at the time of the harvest. Between

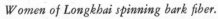

Women of Longkhai spinning bark fiber.

Girls of Wakching carrying water in bamboo vessels.

Girls of Shiong carrying firewood.

the middle of October and the middle of December, when the fields needed little attention, the people of Wakching were engaged in tasks which, for the most part, kept them within the confines of the village. Women spent the days in spinning and weaving, dyeing cloth, making pots, and various other house-based occupations. Men built new houses and repaired old ones; they made a great many baskets and mats and worked in wood, fashioning and carving utensils, implements, and ornaments. Occasionally, they went hunting or fishing. This too was the time when they organized trading expeditions to other villages or went to barter their produce in the markets of the plains.

Even during the period of cultivation, there were days on which no work was done on the fields. Ritual abstention from work was compulsory for all villages at the time of the seasonal feasts and the rites following the bringing in of an enemy head. Eclipses of sun and moon, earthquakes, and certain natural calamities such as devastating storms were followed by days when neither man nor woman might work on the fields. Deaths, funerals, and memorial rites were also occasions when no villager might engage in agricultural pursuits, however pressing the need.

On days of ritual abstention from work, the men undertook no tasks, but for women there were always household duties that had to be performed. Of these, the most irksome, and at the same time the most unavoidable, was the fetching of wood and water. Both spring and woodstore were situated well below the village, and every trip involved a long climb with a heavy load on the back. Since water, at least, had to be fetched even on feast days, women enjoyed far less leisure than men.

2

The Social Structure and Its Units

UNLIKE ETHNIC GROUPS imbued with a strong feeling of tribal identity and solidarity, the Konyaks, though appearing to the outsider as distinct from all neighboring Naga tribes, did not see themselves as a discrete political unit. True, some villages were comprised within confederations under the leadership of a powerful chief, but such groupings were subject to fluctuations in political power and cannot be likened to clearly delimited and permanent tribal units.

The largest corporate social unit was the village. Though divided into wards, which were liable to confront each other in postures of rivalry, a Konyak village evinced on many occasions a spirit of solidarity and considerable local patriotism. Its inhabitants joined in the celebration of the seasonal festivals, performed agrarian rites together, and observed periods of taboo and abstention from work commonly.

Most villages were divided into several quarters or wards, each centered on a morung which gave its name to the ward. The ward was a more closely knit social unit than the village, and we shall see presently that in many respects the morungs of villages acted as separate political units.

Every ward comprised a number of patrilineal, named clans, and these were, in turn, ramified into lineages. The smallest social unit was the household, consisting, usually, of a single nuclear family, but augmented occasionally by a widowed parent or sister of either spouse, or by the orphaned children of a close kinsman.

Across the vertical division of Konyak society into villages, wards, clans, and households, ran a horizontal division into classes of unequal social status. Chiefs, commoners, and an intermediate class formed the elements of this hierarchic order, but the role and respective strength of these status groups differed in the Thenkoh villages and those of the Thendu group. In the former the people of the chiefly class enjoyed few privileges, whereas the powerful chiefs of many

Thendu villages were autocratic rulers whose kinsmen dominated the social and political life of the community. In the language of Wakching the chiefs are described as Ang and the commoners as Ben, and here I shall use only these terms; in most Thendu dialects aristocrats are called Wang, and in the Wanchu dialect the respective terms are Wang and Peng. There is no general term for the class of intermediate status. Angs of pure chiefly blood are invariably described as "great" Angs, whereas the offspring from unions between "great" Angs and women of commoner status rank as "small" Angs, a status which was passed on to their children.

In the following discussion of villages, wards, and clans these terms will be used, although there is a detailed analysis of the position of chiefs in a later section of this chapter.

The Village Community

A Konyak village constituted the framework within which all other social units operated and interacted. Its distinctive identity was often underlined by the use of a language at variance with the dialects of other villages, and certain details of material culture and customary behavior also distinguished one village from the other.

The village was a territorial unit claiming an exclusive right to a clearly delimited tract of land, and in the case of a powerful village also exercising the right of overlordship over a wider territory settled by tributary villages. Only in a very restricted sense could a village be regarded as an economic unit. The village council determined which part of the village land was to be cleared for cultivation, but this was its only major policy decision affecting the economic activities of the community. Agricultural work was not organized at the village level, and communal efforts, as distinct from those made by individual families, always involved the cooperation of the members of a morung or sometimes the members of two morungs which stood in a relationship of reciprocal obligations.

To what extent was a Konyak village a political unit? Villages of the Thendu group, which were ruled by powerful chiefs, invariably faced the outside world as united communities, but in Thenkoh villages the individual morungs often acted independently and there was little solidarity in matters concerning political relations with the inhabitants of other villages.

In Wakching there was a village council consisting of the chief, a shadowy figure, and ten morung officials known as *niengba*. This council adjudicated disputes and punished offences and breaches of taboos concerning the community as a whole. The fines imposed on offenders consisted usually of pigs and rice, and even if a fine was paid in land, the latter was soon sold and converted into pigs and rice beer. All fines were shared between the members of the village council, and those harmed by the offender derived no benefit. Thus, if a man accidentally set fire to a piece of forest, he had to pay a fine of one big basket of rice, which was consumed by the village councilors. The man whose forest got burned received no share in the fine and no compensation. This system of justice discouraged litigation, for whatever the outcome of a case, only the councilors profited from the fines paid.

The village council also decided matters of ritual and ceremony and fixed the dates for communal agricultural rites. In ritual affairs, more than in any others, the village acted as a unit. The seasonal feasts and days of abstention from work (*genna*) were observed simultaneously by all wards of a village, and there were several ritual experts who acted on behalf of the entire village. Thus, in Wakching the *niengba* of one of the five men's houses proclaimed the commencement of agrarian rites throughout the entire village, and when a captured human head was brought in, he performed the rites irrespective of the morung affiliation of the successful head-hunter.

At the times of earthquakes, storms, or other natural disasters the village took joint action to contain or avert the threat of misfortune.

Whereas a village acted vis-à-vis supernatural powers as a unit, it seldom showed a comparable *ésprit de corps* in confronting neighbors or enemies. In Thenkoh villages raids were seldom undertaken by the men of all the morungs. As a rule, only members of one or two men's houses cooperated in a head-hunting expedition. When a village was attacked, its inhabitants would normally join in its defense, but in spite of a strict taboo on actively helping an enemy by fighting members of one's own village, treachery of rival morungs was not unknown. The obligation to revenge a person killed by enemies rested with the members of the victim's clan and morung, not with all his covillagers. Among the Thendu Konyaks, however, the whole village would go to war under the leadership of its chief.

Though most villages appeared to be virtually autonomous units, there existed networks of alliance and patronage linking several villages. In the days of unrestricted warfare and head-hunting, alliances served the purpose of mutual aid, and small villages sought the protection of powerful neighbors. In such cases tribute was paid in return for protection, the amount being determined by the relative strength of the partners. If unable to obtain such protection from friendly neighbors, a weak community might be forced to come to terms with those who had threatened its existence and recognize their overlordship by paying substantial tribute. This was not the only kind of tribute levied. When a village had been built on land belonging to another village, tribute was paid in recognition of the original ownership of the land.

In dealing with its neighbors a large village of the Thenkoh group seldom acted as an undivided entity, and in the sphere of "foreign relations" the individual morungs and their wards rather than the village appeared as the political units.

Wakching, for example, with its 249 houses, had always been a great power. It exercised overlordship over 14 smaller villages, received their tribute, and until the coming of British rule, afforded them a measure of protection. Few of these vassal villages, however, were dependent on Wakching as a whole; most of them were tributaries of one or another of the men's houses.

The majority of these satellites were attached to the Oukheang morung, traditionally the men's house of the founder of Wakching. The value of their tribute varied from a levy of rice payable by every household of the vassal settlement, to a small, purely ceremonial gift in recognition of the traditional dependence. There were, altogether, eleven villages which recognized the overlordship of the Oukheang, and in the majority of cases this recognition was due because the land on which the villages were built had originally belonged to the Oukheang morung. The payments of tribute due to the Oukheang from these eleven villages were as follows:

1. Shiong: One bamboo vessel of husked rice from every household as tribute; the Oukheang men went annually to Shiong and had the right to spear and eat one pig.

2. Totok Chingniu: Three baskets of rice from the whole village as tribute; see also item 3.

3. Totok Chinkok: Three baskets of rice as tribute; when the chief of either of the two Totok settlements died, the Oukheang men were entitled to spear one pig.

4. Tanhai: One bamboo vessel of rice from every household as tribute. Once a year the Oukheang men went to Tanhai and ate one pig; when the chief of Tanhai died, they ate two pigs, each of the two Tanhai morungs providing one pig.

5. Punkhung: Same tribute as Tanhai; on the death of the chief three pigs were eaten, one from each of the three morungs of Punkhung.

6. Longkhai: Same as item 5.

7. Oting: A nominal quantity of rice and a few fish as tribute; once a year the Oukheang men visited Oting and ate one pig; on the death of the chief they ate two pigs.

8. Lunglan: No tribute in rice; the right to one pig annually, usually not exercised because of the great distance; the right to two pigs on the death of the chief.

9. Wangla: No tribute in rice. When the Oukheang morung was rebuilt or a new wooden gong carved, Wangla contributed one buffalo.

10. Lungnyu: No tribute in rice; the right to two pigs on the death of the chief.

11. Lapha: A village founded on Oukheang land in the British period paid an annual fee of five rupees in coins.

The Oukheang men received these payments not so much for their protection, which in the 1930s was no longer necessary, and which in any case must have been difficult to render on account of the great distances between Wakching and the tributary villages, but in consideration of their rights to the land occupied. The Oukheang men were considered the "owners" of the land, and were therefore entitled to receive tribute from those living on it. As the distance from Wakching to Oting is 11 miles, and to Lunglan 15 miles, the Oukheang men admitted that they had never been able to cultivate the land. Yet, the land was theirs, and they insisted that their permission had to be asked before these villages could be established.

It was not unusual for a village to have overlapping obligations to two overlords. Oting and Longkhai, for instance, paid tribute to the Oukheang morung of Wakching, but were also vassals, or, as the Konyaks said, "sons," of Mon, a powerful village whose chiefly family had provided Oting and Longkhai with their chiefs. The paramount chief of Mon was, therefore, the overlord of the chiefs of Oting and Longkhai and received tribute from them. As Mon and Wakching had always been at peace, no conflicting loyalties resulted from the crosscutting of political links, but in other cases the position of a small village between two powerful overlords could become precarious.

In the same way as the smaller villages to the northeast of Wakching were tributary to the Oukheang morung, so several villages to the south recognized the overlordship of the Thepong morung. In the year of my stay in Wakching the Thepong men decided that they would not hire and jointly cultivate any field, on behalf of the morung because the tribute they received from their vassals would provide sufficient rice for all their morung celebrations.

One day in October about thirty men from Chongwe, a village then situated in unadministered territory, brought their tribute to Wakching. After putting down baskets filled with rice in front of the Thepong morung, they were entertained by the Thepong men, and were given substantial quantities of salt as a present. The Wakching people could obtain salt from the plains of Assam, but for the men of Chongwe, who lived too far in the interior to have much trade with the plains, salt was a valuable commodity. By this voluntary gift the Thepong men perpetuated the tribute system, which by that time had become virtually meaningless as far as Chongwe and Wakching were concerned. For Chongwe was, even then, often at war with its neighbors, while Wakching was under British control and the Thepong men were, therefore, hardly in a position to lend armed support to their allies, even had they wished to do so. The sanctity of traditional obligations combined with a desire for trade goods, however, was a sufficiently strong motive to induce the Chongwe men to continue to pay their tribute year after year. The Thepong men felt that the principle of reciprocity had to be maintained even in the changed political situation, and so they substituted gifts of salt for the military aid they could no longer provide.

Not all the men's houses of Wakching received tribute. The only allies of the Bala men were some of the morungs of Wanching, and as that village was of the same size and strength as Wakching, no question of tribute arose. Neither did the Amg-ban exercise overlordship over any other village, but the Ang, in his capacity as chief of Wakching, continued to receive tribute from twelve villages, even though he was a weak and ineffectual man without much influence in his own community, as will be seen later in this chapter, in the section "Chiefs and Commoners." (p. 52)

The alliances linking certain Wakching morungs with other villages was also manifested in an exchange of ceremonial visits. Thus, once a year the Thepong people visited the villages of Chingtang and Chinglong and the people of these villages paid annual return visits to Wakching. When the Thepong men went to Chingtang, they danced with the Chingtang girls, and, similarly, Chingtang men came and danced in the Thepong morung with the daughters and sisters—but never the wives—of the Thepong men. Sometimes the girls of a ward also went on such ceremonial visits and danced with the young men of the host village.

Even on such ceremonial visits, there was an inequality of privilege between overlords and tributaries. While it was the recognized right of the Thepong boys visiting Chingtang to sleep with the girls of that village, a Chingtang man caught in Wakching in a similar adventure with a Thepong girl was fined.

In the days of head-hunting it often happened that the loyalties of a village were divided at morung level, one ward being on friendly and the other on feuding terms with one or all the wards of a neighboring village. Thus, before Wakching came under British administration Punkhung, a tributary of the Oukheang, had a feud with the Balang and Bala morungs of Wakching. This did not mean that there was a great deal of organized fighting, but no Punkhung man would have dared to enter Wakching unless well protected by his Oukheang friends.

When several families of Tanhai, a village tributary to the Oukheang, emigrated from Tanhai to Tamlu, a village south of Wakching, they sought refuge in the Ang-ban ward as they passed through Wakching. The story runs that the Oukheang men had sworn to kill every Tanhai man who tried to leave their zone of influence, but a dense mist obscured the immigrants as they approached Wakching, and they reached the Ang morung undetected. There, they were safe from their infuriated overlords. As the path from Wakching to Tamlu belongs not to the Oukheang but to the Balang and Bala morungs, the Oukheang men could not prevent the Tanhai people from proceeding to Tamlu without provoking a conflict with the other Wakching morungs.

This tradition undoubtedly has a historical basis, for the people of one Tamlu morung still speak the Tanhai language. It highlights, moreover, the strain which the political independence and separate alliances of individual morungs must have on occasion imposed on the unity of a village.

Morungs as Social Units

The analysis of any aspect of Konyak social organization inevitably involves frequent references to the role of the morungs, and it is obvious that a knowledge of their internal structure and their relations with each other is essential for an understanding of the working of Konyak society. We have seen that in the village of Wakching there were five morungs. Their names were Oukheang-ban, Thepong-ban, Balang-ban, Bala-ban, and Ang-ban. The word ban is the Wakching term for morung, but though the villagers invariably spoke of the Ang-ban, which literally means "chief's morung," they usually omitted the syllable ban when talking of the other morungs, and I have here adopted this abbreviated form.

Each of the morungs corresponded to one ward, and in Konyak usage the morung names applied both to the actual men's houses and to the wards of which they were the focal points. Not only men but women as well spoke of belonging to such-and-such a morung, and there was no other term for the divisions of a village which in anthropological usage are described as wards.

The numbers of houses in the five wards of Wakching were as follows: Oukheang, 40; Thepong, 82; Balang, 41; Bala, 45; and Ang-ban, 42. The population of each of these wards was divided between several clans of varying status. The names and the distribution of these clans are listed in the following table:

TABLE 1

	Clans		
Morung	Chiefly (Ang)	Intermediate	Commoner (Ben)
Oukheang	—	—	Shayong-hu
	—	—	Khoknok-hu
	—	—	Yana-hu
Thepong	—	—	Shayong-hu
	—	—	Khoknok-hu
	—	—	Yana-hu
	—	—	Meta-hu
	—	—	Wemnok-hu
Balang	Angnok-pong	—	Yinyong-hu
			Meta-hu
Bala	—	Shungta-hu	Leunok-hu
	—	—	Dzonok-hu
	—	—	Maibang-hu
Ang-ban	Angnok-pong	—	Yinyong-hu
	Nokanok-pong	—	—
	Niamei-hu	—	—

Table 1 shows that some clans were confined to one morung, while others were found in two morungs. This can be explained by the history of the five morungs regarding which traditional accounts were unanimous. The Oukheang morung claimed to be the oldest and associated with the founder of Wakching, who was of Shayong-hu clan. Of almost equal antiquity was the Balang morung, which was also established at the time when Wakching was founded. It is significant that no clan was common to these two original morungs. As the village grew, some Oukheang men built the Thepong, which was considered to be closely related to the Oukheang. Similarly, the Bala was regarded as an offshoot of the Balang. Much later the Ang morung was built under circumstances which cannot be completely reconstructed, but involved probably the acquisition of a chief from another village, a process which was at one time as usual as was the establishment of foreign dynasties in European states of the nineteenth century.

The Wakching morungs were exogamous units, and sexual relations between members of the same morung were considered incestuous. An exception to the rule of morung exogamy was made, however, in the case of people who had either themselves come from other villages, or whose fathers and grandfathers had been immigrants. Though there was a tendency to absorb such aliens into Wakching clans, the process of incorporation took several generations, and first generation immigrants could intermarry freely with the inhabitants of the ward in which they had settled. Similar was the position of the men of the chiefly Angnok-pong clan which lived in the Balang morung. They could marry commoners of their own morung, which suggests that the chiefly clans stood in some respects above and outside the system of morung exogamy.

The individual morungs were not the largest exogamous units. Pairs of morungs, the Oukheang and Thepong on the one side and the Balang and Bala on the other side, constituted larger exogamous units, a situation which seems to have been a logical outcome of the foundation of the Thepong and Bala by members of the two oldest morungs. The members of the Ang-ban, however, intermarried with all the other four morungs. The prohibitions of marriages between clan members remained valid even if a man and a woman bearing the same clan name belonged to two wards which otherwise stood in connubial relations. The Meta clan, for instance, was represented in both the Thepong and the Balang ward, and although people of these wards were normally potential mates, no two members of the Meta clan were allowed to marry.

Insofar as morung activities were concerned, all members of a Wakching morung were equals, irrespective of their class status. There were several officials in every morung who acted on ceremonial occasions, but they had few privileges in daily life.

I have referred already to the *niengba*, the representatives of the morung who, together with the chief, constituted the village council. In some morungs there was only one *niengba*, whereas in others there were two such officials. Their office was hereditary and was handed down from father to son, or, failing a son, to the next agnatic kinsman of suitable age. Some of the *niengba* had special duties. The *niengba* of the Oukheang, a descendant of the village founder, announced the days of the principal village rites, and one of the two *niengba* of the Balang made a similar announcement regarding the performance of a rite to avert pests affecting the crops.

In addition to proclaiming days of ritual rest, the *niengba* of the Oukheang performed the initiation ceremony for all boys entering a morung. Before the suppression of head-hunting it was also his duty to cut off the ears, nose, and tongue of every head brought in and to bury them under a stone in front of the Ang's house.

In most villages there were, in addition, morung officials known as *benba* whose duty it was to kill sacrificial animals at certain rites and to perform functions which were considered magically dangerous, such as the painting of coffins.

On a different level from the *niengba* and *benba* stood the morung chiefs who, like village chiefs, were known as Angs. Their status varied according to the political system in any particular village, and it was only in villages ruled by autocratic chiefs that the morung chiefs were of some importance. There, they received shares of all animals killed at morung rites and were entitled to some free labor from all morung members, but their duties were purely ceremonial.

Members of a morung cooperated in numerous social, economic, and ritual activities. The intimacy prevailing between all the inmates of a men's house facilitated the smooth operation of joint activities and made it possible to dispense with an organization which would have given individuals the power to exercise authority over their fellow members. Even the morung officials were not so much administrators of morung affairs as representatives of the community in its dealings with supernatural powers. Boys who entered the morung at the same time formed an age group whose members worked, danced, and played together until the time when the obligations of family life loosened the close links between members.

The corporateness of a morung community found expression in the joint ownership of a common estate consisting of tangible property as well as of a body of rights. The morung building, the land belonging to a morung, and the well-built, stone-paved path leading to the morung, as well as the stores of grain resulting from cooperative cultivation or received as tribute, were tangible possessions, but there were also numerous intangible rights in which all the members of a morung shared. Among these were the right to specific morung decorations, the right to dance certain dances and sing certain songs "owned" by the morung, the right to sleep with the girls of tributary villages and to kill and eat a specified number of pigs of those same villages. These rights were matched by obligations such as the duty to defend, and, if necessary, avenge, a morung member, to cooperate in the rebuilding of the morung and the cultivation of morung fields, and—in the case of tributary obligations incurred by a morung—to help in raising the annual payments.

In view of all this it is not surprising that a Konyak identified himself with his morung community and showed a deep sense of pride in the might and the glory of his morung.

Clans and Lineages

However strong the sense of loyalty and mutual obligation between the members of a morung may have been, it did not attain the degree of identification and joint responsibility prevailing among those belonging to the same clan. In the language of Wakching a clan is called *li*, but in certain contexts, and especially in the clan names, the syllables *hu* and *phong* attached to the name of the ancestor also mean "clan."

A Konyak clan was a named patrilineal and exogamous descent group whose members considered themselves as consanguineous kin,[1] although descent from the presumptive ancestor and founder of the clan could not be traced in detail. The unity of the clan expressed itself in the fact that at sacrifices and most ritual acts one clan elder functioned for all clan members. This ceremonial representation of clan members by one dignitary was limited only in cases of clans extending beyond the limits of one village ward. In such cases the clan members dwelling within any one ward formed the basic ritual unit.

Even if countless generations had passed since the foundation of a village, each clan still remembered the site on which the founding ancestor had first built his house. On this site stood, as a rule, the house which the clan members regarded as their ancestral home and ritual center. It was called "house of the great elder

---

[1] A group is described as exogamous if its members are debarred from intermarriage and must, hence, "marry out." Consanguineous kin are those related by blood.

brother," and it was assumed that from this house all the remaining houses of the clan, known as "houses of the younger brothers," were founded. Whoever lived in the "great house" was regarded as the head of the clan, and the owners of all houses, founded by younger sons who had separated from the great house, gave him a share of all animals sacrificed at domestic rites.

A concrete example will demonstrate the manner in which the process of branching off from an ancestral house determined the interrelations between the members of a clan. In the Oukheang ward of Wakching there were one great house of the Khoknok-hu clan and fourteen "small houses." The latter, however, had not all been founded by younger brothers of a onetime owner of the great house; some had been established by men who themselves stemmed from small houses. Consequently, the great house received shares of meat from only six houses, which we may call A, B, C, D, E, and F. House A, in turn, received shares of the animals sacrificed by house a, which was an offshoot of A, and this house a, from which four more houses (a, β, γ, δ) had issued, received shares from these four houses. Finally, one of the latter four houses had, in turn, become the parent house of a more recently founded house.

The shares of meat presented by the descendants of younger brothers to the household of the seniormost line were symbolic of a corporateness which involved a high degree of joint responsibility of all members of a lineage with a great house recognized as the apex of the clan. The householder of the great house was ultimately responsible for the debts, fines, and other obligations of all the households which directly or indirectly had branched off from the ancestral house, and they, in turn, collectively stood security for obligations incurred by the great house. The obligations of collective responsibility of kinsmen ran along the same channels as the distribution of shares of meat. Every man was held responsible for the commitments of those households which had branched off from his line, but if he himself was unable to meet them, then the obligations devolved on the household from which his own lineage had sprung. The Konyaks thought of these units not as lines of descent, but as "houses" (*nok*) and the phrases for senior line and junior line were, indeed, "great house" and "small house." Generation after generation would build on the same house site, and such a site symbolized the position of a family in the system of lineages.

Certain positions, such as those of morung officials, were hereditary within the senior lineage of a clan, and succession to such offices went with the inheritance of the great house. On festive days the members of a clan would gather in the great house and there they were entertained with the meat, rice, and rice beer, which the small houses had sent to the great house.

The members of a clan gathered also for the celebration of marriage and the initiation of a boy into the morung community. On that occasion the candidate's father gave a small feast and invited not only the clan members belonging to the same men's house but also clan members residing in other wards.

Cooperation between clan members extended also to economic tasks. A man rebuilding his house was dependent on the labor freely offered by his fellow clansmen, and even when erecting his field huts, he was usually aided by men of his own clan.

Property rights in land could normally be inherited only by persons of the same clan. Though there was—in contradistinction to morung land—no land jointly owned and cultivated by the members of a clan, the prohibition on alienating land to members of different clans, such as to the sons of daughters, suggests that the Konyak clans had some of the features of a property-owning group.

More significant even than the priority of the clan members' claim to the land left by a dead man was the support clan members gave each other in disputes and litigation. In Konyak society, which lacked codified laws and norms, the strength and influence of a litigant's clan were of great importance, for the members of a man's clan gave him their full support, and those who belonged to a small and powerless clan often found it difficult to stand up to the pressure of an opponent supported by a powerful clan. Although the village council would often act impartially and boldly, in doubtful cases the judges usually worked toward a compromise. Under such circumstances, the influence of a powerful clan could sway the deliberations, for the village councilors knew that a decision which left a powerful group resentful did not contribute to the re-establishment of harmony within the community.

An essential characteristic of the clan was its function as the basic exogamous unit. In Wakching, where not only the clans but also the wards were exogamous, this was less apparent than in many other villages, but even here the exogamy of wards was always explained by reference to the brother relationship of the clans they contained.

Although in theory sexual relations between members of the same ward were prohibited, breaches of that rule were not taken very seriously. A love affair between a boy and a girl of the same ward aroused gossip and unfavorable comment, but no public move was made to restrain or discipline the offenders. In the Thepong ward, for instance, there was a man who lived with a woman born in his own ward, though of different clan. Both spouses had been married to persons of the Bala ward, but when widowed, they started to live together. My informants admitted that such a union was shameful, but there was no attempt to boycott the offenders.

The reaction to clan incest was quite different. Sexual intercourse between clan members was considered a crime and traditionally punished by banishment, but in practice the sentence was often modified. In Wakching only one case had occurred in recent years. Yongyong, a man of Bala morung and Leunok clan had committed incest with Shekio, the divorced daughter of his father's brother, who, after leaving her husband, had been given shelter in Yongyong's house. When their love affair became known, both were formally banished. Shekio went to live in Wanching, but Yongyong though forced to abandon his house and his wife, found refuge in the house of a clansman. Later he married another wife and Shekio married a Thepong man and returned to Wakching.

Another case of clan incest occurred in Wanching. There, the ruling chief had sexual relations with a daughter of his father's brother. When the matter became known, his subjects deposed him and exiled the girl. She went to Shiong and subsequently married another man.

In both these cases the villagers gave effect to the rule that clan incest must be punished, but their attitude to the offenders was not vindictive. As soon as incestuous connections had been terminated, the disciplined culprits found people willing to marry them and, after a lapse of time, they were readmitted into village society. Concrete instances of brother-sister incest had not occurred, or at least not come to light, for many generations. There was, however, a legend perpetuating the memory of the passionate love of a brother and a sister, and a song telling of their fate reflects a not altogether unsympathetic attitude to their tragic plight:

> Yinglong and Liwang
> Dearly loved each other,
> Loving they lay together,
> Red as the leaf of the *ou-bou* tree
> Flamed love and desire.
> On the paths to the village,
> The two lit fires,
> Skywards, upwards curling,
> The smoke of the fires united,
> And mingled, never to part.

In this poem the love of Yinglong and her brother Liwang is not condemned but idealized. Happy fulfilment of so unorthodox a passion was impossible and the lovers were doomed, but before they died, they lit fires on two paths leading in opposite directions from Wakching, and the smoke rising in two columns met and mingled over the village, and in it the lovers were united.

The members of a clan had a strong sense of pride in its achievements. Most clans had songs which praised the deeds of past clansmen and acclaimed its superiority vis-à-vis other clans. Such songs often emphasized that the clan had participated in the foundation of the village and that the members were, hence, true descendants of the village founder. Among old established families there was a slight tendency to look down upon later immigrants, and in a quarrel a man was sometimes reminded of his immigrant status.

Yet, there were many newcomers in Wakching, which, as a big and powerful village, had always attracted settlers. Of the eighty-two houses of the Thepong ward eighteen belonged to men who had either immigrated themselves or were descended from men who had come from other villages. Nine of them were originally from Chinglong, one of the villages tributary to the Thepong morung, and the remaining stemmed from Chingtang, Yongwang, and Chi. Those who had themselves moved to Wakching were still regarded as men of their village of origin, but their sons were already incorporated in the one or other of the Wakching clans. It thus appears that recruitment to Konyak clans was not exclusively through the principle of patrilineal descent but also through a mechanism of affiliation. First generation immigrants observed the rule not to marry into the clan which they had joined, but in view of their foreign descent they were allowed to marry girls of other clans of the same ward. The next generation, however, followed entirely the customs of the clan of adoption, and effected a complete assimilation to the local pattern of dress, ornaments, and tattoo.

Such immigrants added to the numerical strength and, hence, the power of the clans which accepted them as affiliated members, and the consideration of these practical advantages must have outweighed the principle that only people of common descent should enjoy the status of fully privileged clan members. In moments of tension, sparked, perhaps, by a purely private quarrel, the latent feeling of superiority of the genuine clan members by descent might have found expression in offensive remarks aimed at the newcomers, but normally original clan members and new recruits lived together in amicable fashion. The heterogeneous composition of many clans certainly did not affect their function as highly important units in the social structure of the village.

Chiefs and Commoners

In a village of the Thenkoh group one could live for a considerable time without being conscious of distinctions of rank or social class. Whether one joined the men who were gossiping and doing odd jobs in the porch of a morung or accompanied a group of families on their way to the fields, all villagers seemed to treat each other as equals, and even on the occasions when rites and ceremonies were performed, people did not group themselves according to inherited status. Neither were there striking differences in the dress and ornaments worn by men and women of different class, though the members of the one or other morung might have a monopoly on some minor element of personal adornment. In a Thendu village, however, even the most casual observer could hardly fail to notice the gulf dividing the powerful chief and his privileged kinsmen from the commoners, who owed him allegiance and free labor, and approached him only in a respectful bowed posture, without ever looking him straight in the face.

Yet, in the villages of both groups society was divided into aristocratic clans, clans of intermediate status, and commoner clans. Whereas in a village such as Wakching the members of chiefly clans enjoyed few tangible privileges, the chief of a large Thendu village wielded the arbitrary power of a true autocrat.

High rank involves obligations, and Konyak chiefs could maintain their eminent position only by preserving the purity of their noble blood. Only from the marriage of a great Ang and a woman of great Ang rank sprang sons entitled to succeed to their father's position. The sons from a great Ang's union with a woman of lower rank were accorded the status of "small" Angs, and none of their progeny could ever regain the status of great Angs. The chiefs of all the more important Thendu villages were of great Ang class, but we shall see that the chiefs of some minor tributary villages were of small Ang rank.

There were many famous chiefly houses among the Konyaks of the Thendu group, and the spheres of influence of the paramount chiefs of Mon and Chi overlapped to some extent with the sphere of the basically democratic Thenkoh village of Wakching. Several of the chiefs I came to know best in 1936 were vassals of the Ang of Mon, a proud and dignified figure, who at that time never moved without a large retinue of retainers and henchmen.

I do not know how much power he or his successor has retained, but in

1962 autocratic chiefs still ruled in the area of the Wanchu group, and the situation in Niaunu, a large village standing in connubial relations with Mon, may serve as an illustration of their position and role. Tradition has it that twelve generations ago Niaunu was founded by Maipupa, a chief of great Ang class, locally described as Wang-ham. Maipupa had originally come from Tsangnu, and the names of eleven chiefs intervening between him and chief Nyek-pong, who ruled in 1962, were remembered; it is doubtful, however, whether this genealogy of the chiefly house is accurate or whether it represents a telescoped selection of the most notable names.

Niaunu became the parent village of four other villages (Niausu, Mintong, Longphong, and Jedua), ruled by scions of the chiefly house. Being agnatic

Left: The chief of Longkhai wearing ceremonial dress. All Konyaks blacken their teeth artificially. Right: The chief of Longkhai dancing in ceremonial dress with spear and dao.

kinsmen,[2] the chiefs of these villages could not intermarry, and beyond this group of Niaunu colonies there were other villages whose chiefs belonged to the same lineage, and were hence also excluded from marriage alliances with the house of the paramount chief of Niaunu. Members of the lineage of the Niaunu chiefly house had, therefore, to seek wives among the daughters of chiefs of other lineages of great Ang status, such as the lineage of the paramount chief of Mon. The domains of some of these lineages lay at distances of more than a day's journey from Niaunu, but for paramount chiefs it was not unusual to enter into marriage alliances with rulers of far away villages.

The manner of extending a chief's influence over neighboring villages is demonstrated by the establishment of Mintong, one of the four colonies of Niaunu. Originally, the site of the present village of Mintong was occupied by Zonlong, a village ruled by a chief of a lineage different from that of Niaunu. It belonged to a group of villages dominated by Pangchao, whose chiefs stand now in affinal relations to those of Niaunu. Seven generations ago a force of Niaunu warriors raided and defeated Zonlong, wiping out the chief's family, most of the other members of both great and small chiefly clans, and about fifty percent of the commoners. The surviving commoners chose to remain in the village under the new chief, who belonged to a junior branch of the lineage of the paramount chief of Niaunu, and under the new name of Mintong the village was incorporated within the domain of Niaunu.

If the family of the chief of a tributary village became extinct, the paramount chief of the domain would send one of his sons or a brother's son of great Ang rank to take over the vacant position, but as the number of men of pure chiefly blood was usually small, the chief's families being no more immune from the general high mortality rate than other families, a parent village often had no suitable candidate of great Ang rank available, and the villagers were forced to search for a chief in other friendly villages. Thus in 1952 Longsom, a colony of Chanu, but politically allied to Niaunu, could not obtain a chief from Chanu when their chiefly lineage died out. The villagers requested the chief of Niaunu to send them one of his kinsmen, and he obligingly seconded his father's younger brother's son to the chiefdom of Longsom.

The installation of a foreign lineage of chiefs as rulers of a village did not always provide permanent political stability, and Konyak history contains many examples of chiefs who failed to gain the loyalty of their new subjects. The following occurrence involving several Thendu villages in the vicinity of Wakching illustrates the difficulties involved in changing the leadership of a village.

When some fifty years ago the chief of Hangnyu, a village northeast of Wakching, died, a dispute arose over the succession. By right his eldest son, Auwang, should have become chief, but he was so young that his father's brother tried to displace him. The quarrel within the chiefly family endured so long that the other men of chiefly clan and the village elders approached the powerful Ang of Chi, asking him to second one of his brothers as Ang of Hangnyu. The Ang of Chi, however, was too shrewd a statesman to accede to this request. He pointed

---

[2] Agnatic kinsmen are those descended from a common ancestor in the male line.

out that the ruling house of Hangnyu was not extinct and that to add a new chief to the two existing claimants would only aggravate the situation. The people of Hangnyu, however, anxious to set their affairs in order, sent a message to the paramount chief of Pomau, a large village northwest of Niaunu, and he, less cautious than the Ang of Chi, seconded his ambitious brother Kiwang to the chiefdom of Hangnyu.

At first all went well for the new Ang of Hangnyu. He led his subjects successfully against the neighboring village of Tang, and this raid gained Hangnyu a large number of heads, but a few years later his luck began to turn. Kiwang's wife, a daughter of the chiefly house of Mon, died, and so did her only son. Though Kiwang had numerous other children from wives of lower status, none of them were eligible to succeed him, and, thus, there was once more speculation as to the succession of the chieftainship of Hangnyu. This misfortune was followed by a series of poor harvests, which so depleted the wealth of the village that Kiwang found it difficult to provide the necessary sacrificial animals for the celebration of the seasonal rites. Moreover, Tang warriors, reversing the fortunes of war, ambushed a party of Hangnyu people and captured nine heads.

The villagers blamed Kiwang for these misfortunes, for just as the magical virtue of a sacred chief was believed to benefit his subjects, so the ill-luck of a community was ascribed to a decline in the chief's power. The sons of the former chief of Hangnyu, now grown to manhood, took advantage of the discomfiture of the man whom they considered a usurper. They instigated the villagers to ignore his orders, to pay only scanty tribute, and to neglect the work on his fields. Finally, they challenged Kiwang's authority by ostentatiously taking possession of the right hind leg of a buffalo sacrificed at the rebuilding of a morung, a share considered traditionally the prerogative of the village chief.

Kiwang felt that his days in Hangnyu were numbered, and sent messengers secretly to his brother, the powerful Ang of Pomau, asking whether he should withdraw from Hangnyu or whether he could depend on the support of his kinsmen to maintain his position. The Ang of Pomau counseled patience. He could not openly interfere in a village lying outside his domain, but he promised to invite the arrogant Ang sons to a feast in Pomau and to have them murdered. The plot was, however, betrayed, only one of the Ang sons accepted the invitation and he went to Pomau with a large escort of warriors, who took care never to let their weapons out of their hands. Immediately on their return to Hangnyu, the rightful heir to the chieftainship ousted Kiwang and banished him from the village.

However, the story did not end there. With Kiwang, many followers and servants had come to Hangnyu. They had acquired fields and built houses, and their sons and daughters had grown up in Hangnyu. Were they now to return as landless refugees to Pomau? No, they had made their homes in Hangnyu and wanted to remain Hangnyu people. "Well, if you are Hangnyu men why don't you fetch us a few heads from Pomau?" Though spoken mockingly, these words were taken seriously by four of Kiwang's onetime followers. On a moonless night they crept into Pomau and killed an unsuspecting couple sleeping on the veranda of a granary; but hardly had they severed the heads of the luckless lovers when a sentry gave the alarm, and the Pomau warriors set out in pursuit of the raiders.

Only one escaped; two were overtaken and killed, and the fourth fled into the forest and climbed a high tree in the hope of putting his pursuers off the scent. In the morning the Pomau warriors discovered him, and surrounded the tree, but the situation was tricky. In the darkness of night, they had reacted to the attack by killing two men of whose identity they were ignorant. In the light of day they found, however, that the fugitive in the tree was one of their own kinsmen. Though his crime, which violated the most sacred bonds of village solidarity, had to be punished, their hands were tied by the taboo forbidding the shedding of the blood of a covillager. For the followers of Kiwang belonged to the chiefly clan of Pomau, and though they had emigrated to Hangnyu, they counted as Pomau men.

There was only one way to end the unprecedented situation. The Ang of Pomau himself had to intervene, for his status allowed him to disregard taboos with impunity, and his magical power was so great that not even the killing of a man of his own village could harm him. So the old Ang climbed into a neighboring tree and shot the offender with his muzzle-loader.

The taboo on the killing of agnatic kinsmen and covillagers did not extend to affines[3] living in a different village. A marriage alliance linking two chiefly houses was no guarantee of permanent peace between the domains concerned, and in many cases intermarriage alternated with warfare. In a recent feud between Niaunu and the village of Ninu, for instance, the son of a Ninu woman married in Niaunu was killed by Ninu warriors, that is, by men of his mother's natal village.

Disputes between spouses of chiefly blood sometimes gave rise to feuds involving their respective villages. Some thirty-five years ago a daughter of the chief of Mintong was married to a man of great Ang class of Ninu village. They quarreled and her husband sent her back to Mintong. Although her father was able to arrange her marriage to a kinsman of the Ang of Pomau, the men of the chiefly clan of Mintong felt insulted, and prepared to raid Ninu. The Ninu warriors, however, forestalled the raid and, ambushing Mintong men, captured six heads. Then all the villagers of the Niaunu domain, to which Mintong belonged, joined in a raid on Ninu and captured three heads.

This feud would probably have continued if the country had not been brought under the control of the government of India. Years later those villagers who had lost kinsmen in the fighting still remembered the unresolved feud and did not accept food in the houses of the killers or of their descendants.

The role of chiefs in war was ambiguous. Some chiefs participated personally in raiding parties, but there was some feeling that a man killing a ruling chief of great Ang rank incurred magical dangers. As a rule, a chief would not be killed in an unprovoked ambush or, indeed, in a fight at the beginning of hostilities, but once fighting had escalated, even a chief might be killed in battle. Some of my informants thought that the hesitation to kill the chief of a hostile village was due more to the fear of retaliation than to that of the possible magical ill-effects. Yet, the people of Wakching definitely believed that chiefs of great Ang class radiated dangerous magical powers. A special illness, of which severe headache and pain in the eyes were the symptoms, was attributed to contact with

---

[3] Affines are kinsmen related by marriage.

great Angs. The chiefs did not suffer from this illness themselves, but they caused it in others. Many Wakching people were therefore afraid to enter a great Ang's house, to look into his eyes, and, above all, to oppose him in any way. They believed that a person arousing an Ang's anger would automatically fall ill.

Both the political and the magical powers of Angs discouraged people of lower status from crossing them. Angs of villages such as Mon and Chi were in the habit of taking by force and with impunity any commoner girl of their domain whom they fancied. They would send men to bring the girl to their house at night and paid no bride price to the parents. If indulged in to excess, such practices would arouse the wrath of a chief's subjects, and it was not unheard of for a chief who had proven unduly overbearing to be assassinated.

There was also the possibility of deposing a chief guilty of a grave offense. Naiwang, the chief of Wanching, committed incest with his father's brother's daughter, who had returned to live in his house after she had been divorced by her husband. When the incestuous relationship was discovered, the villagers deposed Naiwang and installed his father's younger brother's son in his place. Despite the seriousness of the offense, the deposed Ang was allowed to remain in the village, though he had to leave his house and move to a different ward. Wanching belonged to the Thenkoh group of villages, in which chiefs share power with the elders of morungs, and it is possible that a powerful Ang of a Thendu village might have been able to hush up even a case of incest.

The implied sexual prowess of some chiefs was remarkable. Nyekpong, the chief of Niaunu, who in 1962 was a handsome slender middle-aged man of great dignity and charm, had two wives of aristocratic birth. In addition, he had taken twenty-four wives of commoner status, twelve from his own village and twelve from the tributary village of Niausa, but in 1962 only seven of these commoner wives were alive. His father had had twenty wives, two of whom were the daughters of ruling chiefs of other villages.

The class composition of Niaunu was typical of many of the villages of the Thendu group. There were four classes known as Wangham (great Ang), Wangsa (small Ang), Wangsu (intermediate), and Wangpeng (commoner).

The great Ang class consisted exclusively of those members of the ruling chief's lineage who were the issue of marriages between men of great Ang class and women from other villages of similar status. As marriage within the Ang lineage of the same village was inadmissible, all alliances in which both spouses were of great Ang rank had to be contracted with chiefly houses of other domains. Men of great Ang class could marry secondary wives of Wangpeng clans, and the issue from such chief-commoner unions constituted the Wangsa or small Ang class. Girls of great Ang class were never married to commoners of their own village. Ideally, they had to marry men of great Ang lineage of other villages, but if no husband of equal status could be found, they were given in marriage to men of small Ang lineages; these too had to be unrelated and, hence, of another village, for it seems that in the same locality two different lineages of great Ang class never coexisted.

Men of small Ang rank could either marry wives of similar status from other villages or conclude unions with commoner girls of their own village. The children from both types of marriage were of small Ang status, for no further lowering of status by repeated admixture of commoner blood detracted from a one time great Ang ancestor.

There was three named clans of Wangsu or intermediate status in Niaunu. Their members could either marry commoners of their own village or members of clans of Wangsu status from other villages. Some named Wangsu clans occurred in several villages, and in such cases the rules of clan exogamy had to be followed even though the various lineages of one clan might have resided in different villages for many generations.

There were numerous Wangpeng clans in Niaunu. Such commoner clans of the same village could not intermarry, and their members either married commoners of neighboring villages or people of Wangsu clans, who could be of Niaunu or any other village. Women of commoner status were, of course, available as secondary wives of the men of chiefly rank, and such hypergamous unions[4] were a frequent occurrence.

In many villages there were fewer commoners than members of the three higher classes, and it would therefore be misleading to think of Wanchu society in terms of the domination of a small privileged class over a large working population of commoner status. Only the great Ang clan was numerically limited, and this was due to the fact that the offspring of great Ang males and women of any other class were not recognized as of great Ang status, but were incorporated into the small Ang class.

Yet, there was a custom which seemed to make nonsense of the great Angs' claim to the purity of their line. A chief's bride of equal status conformed to the general custom and did not move into her husband's house after the marriage rites, but remained in her parental village, paying occasional visits to her husband. As long as she resided in her natal village, she was allowed to associate with the boys of her own village, and her husband could neither prevent her from having extramarital adventures nor had he any redress if she became pregnant from a man of nonaristocratic status. Such paternity received no social recognition; any child born to a great Ang woman married to a great Ang was considered to be of great Ang rank. The period of a young wife's untrammeled license lasted only as long as she remained in her parents' home; once she resided permanently with her husband, any intrigue with another man was punished as adultery.

The most striking difference between the three upper classes and the commoners lay in the appearance of the women. Those of the two chiefly classes as well as women of intermediate class wore their hair long, whereas all commoner women, even those married to the paramount chief, had their heads shaved or closely cropped.

People of different class did not eat from the same platter, but this taboo on interdining did not mean that the food cooked by one of inferior status could not be eaten by those of higher rank, nor that members of different status did not eat in each other's presence. In a polygamous chief's household there was usually

---

[4] A hypergamous marriage is the union of a man of higher rank with a woman of lower status; marriages of women of higher rank with men of lesser status are described as "hypogamous."

one wife of commoner status who cooked for the chief and his wife or wives of chiefly class. This woman was in charge of the kitchen and it was she who distributed the grain which other wives cooked for themselves on their own hearths.

There were certain restrictions of diet observed by the different classes. Commoners were allowed to eat all animals except tiger, but the higher classes abstained from the flesh of goat and bear.

When an animal was required for public sacrifice, villagers of all classes contributed to the purchase price, but the four classes received unequal shares of the meat, for the chief and the other men of great Ang rank received preferential treatment.

Such a privilege was only the outward expression of the powerful position of the chiefs of great Ang class. Some autocratic rulers exerted an overriding influence over political affairs within their domains and derived great economic benefit from their position as chiefs.

In Niaunu men and women of all households, including those of great Ang class, gave their labor free for the cultivation of the chief's land, and only on certain days did he provide the workers with food and drink. They helped to fell the jungle for his new fields, and to prepare the soil for the rice seed, which the chief himself sowed. He was also entitled to call the villagers to work on his fields at the time of weeding and harvesting. For assistance in certain tasks, such as the cutting up of millet straw or the clearing of weeds from old fields, the paramount chief of Niaunu was accustomed to summon the people of tributary villages, and in return for their labor he fed them meat and rice.

A chief's subjects also cooperated in building his house, and the houses of some chiefs were of impressive size. At the time of my earlier fieldwork the house of the Ang of Hangha measured over 360 feet in length. The interiors of such houses contained great halls comparable to those of a morung, which were used for similar purposes, as well as a great many dark little rooms inhabited by the chief's numerous wives and children. In the room in which the chief received guests stood a carved bench, decorated sometimes with carvings of hornbill heads, and on this "throne" none but the chief might sit.

Among most Naga tribes high social status could be gained by the giving of feasts of merit, but among Konyaks there was only limited scope for the attainment of prestige by public displays and the perpetuation of such achievements by outward symbols. No individual effort in the quest for social advancement was allowed to cancel or blur the unalterable distinction between chiefs and commoners, and no individual could ever cross the class barrier.

The chiefs of the Thendu group, however, did perform rites suggestive of feasts of merit whereby they sought to raise their personal prestige. There were four stages in these rites. The first involved the carving and dragging in of a log gong for the chief's house. When the gong had been brought to the village and placed before the chief's house, chiefs of numerous allied and friendly villages were invited to a great feast. Several mithan (*Bos frontalis*) and buffaloes were sacrificed, and shares of the meat were distributed to the guests. The feast ended with dancing, and on the following day the young men of the chief's village went to the forest and felled trees suitable for the fashioning of forked posts. As many of such Y-posts were carved as animals had been ritually slaughtered. These posts were erected in front of the chief's house, and as this was done, the chief's priest, invariably a man of commoner clan, poured beer on the forked posts and addressed the dead animals with words such as these: "Mithan, buffaloes, do not grieve; in your place we erect these posts; in the future mithan will be as numerous as the eggs of insects." Small pieces of meat from the sacrificial animals were then "fed" to the Y-posts.

At the next feast a large post carved with hornbill motifs was brought in. The men carrying the post chanted in imitation of a tiger's roar "because chiefs are of tiger clan." In front of the chief's house a deep pit was dug, and in this a dog and a cock were placed and crushed as the men slip the post into the hole. As soon as the post stood erect, large numbers of cattle were brought for sacrifice, the slaughter of up to forty mithan being allegedly not unusual.

Both the carving and bringing in of a log gong and the erection of a carved post in front of the chief's house could be repeated in the course of two even more lavish and elaborate feasts. Chiefs who had performed any of these feasts of merit had so gained in power and status that thereafter they were permitted to eat only the purest food. No animal which had been killed or wounded by a beast of prey or which had any blemish, such as a torn ear, was suitable food for chiefs who had performed these feasts of merit.

In Niaunu the chief, supported by the men of great Ang rank, was in control of village affairs. When a breach of customary law occurred in the village, he sent two messengers, who were never of chiefly rank, to apprehend the culprit. Then he summoned all the men of great and small Ang class as well as three commoners who held office as priests and ritual experts. Presiding over this gathering, the chief questioned the offender and witnesses, collected evidence, and consulted with the members of his council. Punishments were usually in the form of fines, and a chief also had the right to fine any man who had refused to obey his orders. An offender who had been warned and fined several times, but had failed to mend his ways, could be sentenced to death. At it was taboo to kill a man or woman of the same village with a weapon, criminals under sentence of death were bound and thrown into a river to drown. Members of the great Ang class were not exempt from such punishment if the seriousness of their crime warranted the death sentence.

My informants recalled three cases of execution by drowning which had occurred in Niaunu. One of the criminals was a habitual thief, one had killed several calves belonging to other men and secreted the meat in his house, and the third had been accused of torturing his own daughter because she had had a lover of whom he did not approve. No concrete case of incest was remembered, but the general view was that a couple guilty of brother-sister incest would suffer death by drowning. Chiefs dealt with unfaithful wives in similar manner. Thus San-wang, the father of the present chief of Niaunu, sentenced two of his commoner wives and their lovers of intermediate rank to death, and had all four drowned in the Tisa river. I was told that notwithstanding the license allowed to a chief's aristocratic bride, as long as she resided in her parental home, a wife of great Ang class who was caught in adultery after she had taken up residence in her husband's house might also have been killed by drowning.

If a dispute occurring in a tributary village could not be resolved by the local chief and his council, the paramount chief of the domain was invited to give judgment and his verdict was final.

The fines imposed by a chief and his council were normally shared between the chief and the members of chiefly clan, but in cases where a complainant had suffered loss or injury, as in the case of theft, he would receive a substantial share in compensation. This was a principle at variance with the practice in Wakching, where compensation was rarely awarded (see discussion earlier in this chapter, in the section "The Village Community").

Disputes over field boundaries were not brought before the chief's council, but were settled informally by all the men of Ang class, and there was no appeal against their decision. This was the practice even in villages such as Oting, where the great Ang class was not represented and the village chief was himself of small Ang status.

In Oting there were about equal numbers of commoners and people of aristocratic clans, and it was normal for these classes to intermarry. Only the sons and daughters of the village chief were expected to marry spouses of equal status from other villages. All other members of chiefly rank were content to marry commoners of their own village, and no preferences were expressed for hypergamous in contrast to hypogamous unions. Marital unions across class lines were thus considered the norm, and facilities in the form of a meeting ground for young men and girls of different class were provided. The chief's house contained one room where the girls of Ang class entertained the boys of commoner clans, and another room in which commoner girls gathered and were visited by boys of Ang class. It is remarkable that despite the fact that, with the exception of the lineage of the village chief, aristocrats and commoners were natural marriage partners, the distinction in privileges and obligation of the classes persisted.

At first sight the marriage system of Thendu villages may appear as totally different from that of a Thenkoh village such as Wakching. Closer analysis, however, reveals a considerable area of agreement. The exogamy of clans is basic to the marriage system of both groups, but whereas in Wakching the wards represent the next larger exogamous unit, among Thendu Konyaks and Wanchus it is the village which constitutes an exogamous unit in respect of all persons of equal status. Thus, a village such as Oting or Niaunu compares to the exogamous units formed in Wakching by a combination of two kindred morungs such as Oukheang and Thepong. And just as in Wakching members of a chiefly clan could intermarry with commoners of *their own ward* in disregard of the general rule of ward exogamy, so in Thendu villages members of different classes could, and often did, intermarry within one and the same village; but whereas in Wakching intraward marriages between aristocrats and commoners were rare exceptions, in villages such as Oting marriages between persons of chiefly status and commoners were the rule, and viewed from the village perspective, this situation appears almost as an instance of "class exogamy." Such an interpretation would be misleading, however, for members of all three classes freely intermarry with persons of their own class provided they belong to different villages and, hence, not to the same clan or to clans standing in a "brother" relationship.

We may wonder whether a system of repeated intermarriage between aristocrats and commoners is not inconsistent with an ideology which sees society as constituted by two or more socially distinct classes. Are we justified in correlating the division of the Konyak tribe into the two cultural groups known as Thenkoh and Thendu with the contradistinction between two political systems, one of which can be labeled "democratic" and the other "monarchic," or should we regard Konyak society as a continuum in which "democratic" and "monarchic" systems merge one into the other and such characteristic institutions as the morung with its age groups have shown themselves capable of adjustment to either system?

There seem to have been many fluctuations between the "democratic" and the "autocratic" system of village government. The decline of a local lineage of chiefs often brought democratic forces to the fore, however, there are instances of villages run on more or less democratic lines inviting outsiders of chiefly blood to assume the position of village chief. The history of the chiefs of Wakching, though somewhat obscure, provides an example for such an event. Toward the end of the nineteenth century the chieftainship of Wakching was held by a lineage of great Ang class, and my informants still remembered the names of Ngamwang and his successor Dzemang. When the latter died without issue, Pongyong, of the chiefly lineage of Tanhai village, succeeded to the chieftainship and married Dzemang's widow, who was of great Ang rank. She died, however, without male offspring, and Pongyong then married a commoner from whom he had several sons. In Pongyong's time trouble broke out between the five morungs of the village, and the quarrel assumed such serious proportions that the four morungs Oukheang, Thepong, Balang, and Ang-ban decided to expel the men of the Bala morung, who were regarded as the troublemakers. Since it was taboo to take up arms against people of one's own village, the four morungs arrayed against the Bala sent messengers to the paramount chief of Chi, asking him to do the job for them and to drive out the Bala men. The traditional democratic order based on the equilibrium of morungs, had broken down, and the chief of Wakching was powerless to restore order. The Ang of Chi agreed to comply with the request of the majority of Wakching morungs, but only on the condition that the Wakching people should depose their own chief and replace him by a member of the chiefly house of Chi. This was conceded, and "in the name of the Ang of Chi" and with the help of some Chi warriors, the men of the four morungs burned the entire Bala ward and drove out the inhabitants. Some Bala people found refuge in Wanching, while others were, surprisingly, allowed to return and were given shelter by individual Balang families under the pretext that they had "become Balang men."

Pongyong was deposed and Longmei, a younger brother of the Ang of Chi, was installed as chief of Wakching and given the land of the previous chief. Pongyong was, however, allotted some land of the expelled Bala men, and was made "morung chief" of the Balang ward. Only many years later, when Wakching came under British administration, were the Bala people permitted to re-establish their ward and rebuild their morung.

It would seem that Longmei never succeeded in imposing as autocratic a rule on Wakching as that exercised by the chiefs of Chi in their own domains, and that the Wakching morungs always retained some of their independence. Neither did circumstances favor the growth of a powerful chiefly house. Longmei's only wife of great Ang class and all her four children died, and although he had five other wives, his only surviving son was the offspring of a woman of commoner status. This son, Chinkak, ranked, therefore, as a small Ang. He nevertheless succeeded his father as chief of Wakching, but had neither the status nor the personality to rule effectively. At the time of my stay in Wakching Chinkak was chief only in name; he had been addicted to opium eating[5] for years and had sold most of his land. Despite the decline in his fortunes, the villagers continued to give him free labor and such shares of meat as were due to a ruling chief, and he continued to receive tribute from some of Wakching's vassal villages.

Though neither the village chief nor the members of other clans of chiefly rank enjoyed positions comparable to that of the aristocrats in such villages as Chi, Mon, and Niaunu, the status difference between commoners and aristocrats was never disputed by the commoners who formed the majority of the people of Wakching, and among whose ranks were some of the richest and most influential men of the village. They conceded without hesitation the right of the members of chiefly clans to marry several wives, while accepting that monogamy was mandatory for commoners. Thus, double standards of morality appeared even to commoners as a natural concomitant of a society structured on hierarchic lines.

A greater knowledge of the history of individual villages might well lead to a reappraisal of the apparent distinction between the democratic tendencies of most Thenkoh villages and the monarchic rule observable among the Konyaks of the Thendu group. There are many indications that the dividing line between the two systems has been fluid, and it would seem that historic accident, such as the personality of a chief or the extinction of a chiefly lineage, could have brought about a swing from the one system to the other.

A similar case of the coexistence of two contrasting types of political organization within an area of considerable cultural homogeneity has been reported from the Kachins, the neighbors of the Nagas on the eastern side of the Indo-Burma border. In *Political Systems of Highland Burma* (1954) E. R. Leach has discussed this problem in great detail, and his conclusions are very relevant to the evaluation of the Konyak case. Seen against the background of the situation among the hill people of Burma, the Thenkoh-Thendu dichotomy appears as an extension of a known and widespread pattern of fluctuating systems of tribal government and not as a freak combination of irreconcilable political ideologies and practices. Neither is the rigid division of Thendu society into hereditary classes of unequal status without parallel among the peoples of the North East

---

[5] Some Konyaks mix opium with the tobacco used for chewing and thus "eat" it; others smoke it mixed with tobacco.

Frontier Agency. The Apa Tani tribe in the mountains north of the Brahmaputra consists also of a privileged upper class and a lower stratum composed of commoners and slaves, but despite this hierarchic order, there is among the Apa Tanis no institution of chieftainship, and the system of village government is basically democratic.[6] In Burma, however, powerful dynasties of chiefs occur not only among the Kachins but also among Chins, and in the context of such traditions of social stratification the Konyak system of hereditary chiefs can be understood much more easily than if we looked upon it as an unusual variant of the social order prevailing among the other Naga tribes.

[6] See my book *The Apa Tanis and their Neighbours*, London, 1962.

┌───────┐
│   3   │
└───────┘

Phases of Life

THE DIFFERENCES IN THE POLITICAL SYSTEMS of the various sections of the Konyak tribe did not affect all aspects of social behavior to the same degree, and it is possible, therefore, to discuss such subjects as the education of children, the conduct of the unmarried, and the relations of spouses without distinguishing in every case between customs peculiar to specific localities or groups of villages. The following pages contain a general account of the progress of Konyaks from conception through childhood, adolescence and maturity to death, and the passage into the land of the dead. Though examples are taken from various villages, the greater part of the description reflects life in Wakching as I observed it in 1936–1937.

Pregnancy and Birth

The basic facts of the sexual functions were known to the Konyaks, and it was recognized that a single act of sexual intercourse was sufficient to cause conception. There was a widespread belief, however, that a child in the womb would be weak and unhealthy if it was not reinforced by repeated copulation. Contraceptive devices or practices were unknown, and the people of some villages and particularly those of Wakching were emphatic in their condemnation of attempts to bring on abortion.

The duration of a pregnancy was fairly accurately predicted, though some Konyaks thought that women impregnated by men of chiefly class carried a child for ten months, while the pregnancies of the wives of commoners lasted only nine months. The natal class of the woman was considered irrelevant for the duration of a pregnancy.

During the period of gestation, a woman was not allowed to eat the meat of buffaloes or mithan, because of the fear that the child might be born with horns, and she had to abstain from pork because sows were given to eating their own placentas. She was also forbidden to eat the flesh of birds caught in traps because if she did so the child might be imprisoned in the womb at the time of delivery. The husband of a pregnant woman was also subject to various taboos. He was not permitted to touch or cut up a dead animal, and was not supposed to make baskets or set traps for birds.

The first confinement of every woman took place in her parents' house. Her mother, if she was still alive, and another old woman of the mother's clan acted as midwives. If labor was unduly protracted, it was assumed that the woman's husband had broken one of the taboos which he should have observed during his wife's pregnancy. All baskets present in the house were torn to bits in order to facilitate, by sympathetic magic, the release of the trapped child. Moreover, a chicken was sacrificed to Gawang, the sky god, with a prayer for the opening of the womb.

Only women and very old men remained in a house in which a woman was giving birth. The husband was never permitted to be present, even at the birth of a second or subsequent child which took place in his own house, but he was not supposed to leave the village. In the village of Oting it was customary for all males, even small boys, to leave the house of birth, and for six days they slept and ate in the houses of kinsmen. All the husband's weapons were removed from the house, for if they remained he would have no luck in the chase.

After her first confinement a woman left her parental house and went as soon as possible, often within hours, to the house of her husband. The next day the oldest man of the husband's clan sacrificed one or two chickens and gave the child a name. Soon afterward the kinswomen of the young mother visited the house to ask what the child was called. Each brought a load of firewood in order to make provision for the days when the mother would be unable to fetch wood herself. However, a Konyak mother's period of rest was short. On the fourth day after confinement she went to the spring to bathe, and soon afterward she resumed her domestic duties.

The house containing the newborn child was closed to strangers from other villages for six days, and people from distant villages beyond the river were not permitted to enter it for one whole month. To prevent the accidental entrance of strangers, the house of the newborn child was marked with a symbol—a bunch of leafy bamboos in the case of a boy, and a branch of cane if the newborn was a girl.

The idea underlying this custom was apparently not the fear of pollution connected with childbirth, but the belief that a newborn child was particularly vulnerable to dangerous influences emanating from strangers.

Konyaks were, on the whole, not pollution conscious. Menstruating women continued their normal activities and cooked for their husbands and families. Married couples normally abstained from sexual intercourse for five days, but not from any fear of pollution, and unmarried girls were sometimes persuaded to sleep with their lovers even at the time of menses.

Childhood

At birth a child belonged to the clan of the man who, as the husband of its mother, was regarded as the child's legal father. There was no rite of formal acceptance into the father's clan, but every Konyak child enjoyed from the moment of birth the protection of the members of the clan to which the mother's husband belonged.

We shall see later that the clan membership of a child could be changed if the mother left her legal husband and, subsequently, married the man whom she regarded as the biological father, and who would accept the child as his own. In this case, however, it was not biological paternity but the mother's marriage which determined the child's clan membership and its position in the social system. Only in the rare case of a child born to an unmarried girl did the biological paternity automatically determine the child's clan membership. On no account could a child belong to the mother's natal clan.

Children were generally welcomed and treated with care and tenderness by both parents. The first months of infancy were spent mainly on the backs of parents and elder siblings. Usually, a Konyak woman resumed work on the fields a few days after her confinement, and wherever she went, she carried the baby. During breaks in field work she would feed the child, and when she returned to the village in the evening, she handed it to her husband while she prepared the evening meal. When a child was several months old and no longer entirely dependent on the mother's milk, it was left in the village in the care of an old kinswoman or of older brothers and sisters.

Soon a small boy or girl would learn to move about the village, and though children were not characterized by particular docility, they knew very well how far they could go without running into trouble; it was most unusual for a child to stray into the jungle surrounding the village. Usually, children respected the limits of their own village ward, and this had the result that their companions at play belonged almost exclusively to the same morung.

Children played in groups divided by sex, and the older they grew, the more noticeable this division became. There was no definite rule which forbade the boys to play with their sisters and female cousins, but in practice one never saw boys and girls in one play group.

With large numbers of children left day after day to their own devices, one might have expected the development of numerous organized games, but there were, in fact, very few, and the only real toys were tops, which the boys spun with great skill, trying to hit and upset the tops of other players.

While the boys had no imitative games, small girls played with dolls crudely made of rags or with the seeds of sword beans, which they used as missiles in a stone-hitting game.

The scarcity of children's games may partly have been due to the children's early integration into the adult community, and their active participation in economic activities at a comparatively tender age. There was no need to build a world of their own, for they shared the world of their parents, and adults had few interests which lay beyond the comprehension of children. Young children were treated as reasonable and responsible persons, and there were few opportunities for coercion or punishment of naughy children. During my entire stay among the Konyaks I saw only one child beaten, and this beating was nothing more than a few slaps which an angry grandmother gave to a screaming little boy who refused to leave the fascinating spectacle of house-building and go and eat his dinner. Parents spoke to their children in the same quiet and friendly tone they would use to adults. A grumbling father, shouting at his children in public, would have been subject to the disapproval of his kinsmen and neighbors, and parents reacted to minor acts of indiscipline with tolerance and apparent indifference.

Yet, despite this permissive attitude of parents, Konyak children soon grew into responsible members of the community. Two factors promoted this development: the children's early integration into the economic life and the education which the boys received in the morung.

The time of carefree days spent at play with agemates in the deserted village and of evenings, nights, and mornings in the cosy atmosphere of the parental home drew to an end when a boy reached his eighth or ninth year. At this age he was already familiar with his father's morung, where he had often played when the great hall was empty and most men were at work in the fields, but now, he became a member of the morung in his own right and, henceforth, spent his nights in the company of the unmarried boys and men.

Entry into the morung community bore all the signs of an initiation rite which marked the passage from childhood to adolescence, and established a boy in the rights and duties of a morung member.

In Wakching this initiation ceremony was always performed in October, shortly after the end of the harvest, when people had time for the celebration of feasts. In the year of my stay in Wakching it was performed only by the people of the Thepong morung, for only in this morung were there sufficient boys of a suitable age, that is, between the ages of seven and ten.

Six days after the new moon the boys and girls of the Thepong went to the jungle to collect wild herbs and the soft shoots of wild banana plants, for vegetables from the jungle, and not those which were cultivated, were the proper food for the initiation feast. The next day Yonglong, the descendent of the village founder and priest (*niengba*) of the Oukheang morung, went to the houses of the six Thepong boys who were to be initiated. In each of the houses he was entertained with rice and rice beer, and then a sacrificial animal, a pig by rich and a chicken by poorer families, was killed in front of the house. The killing was done by the oldest man of the boy's clan, and the same man blessed the boys and prayed for their welfare.

Little else happened on that day, but the boys as well as the girls of the families, celebrating the initiation of their sons, alternated in beating the giant wooden gong of the morung.

On the morning of the next day, the parents of the candidates entertained all the members of their clan with large quantities of food and rice beer. As a contribution toward the expense of the feast, every guest brought one bamboo vessel filled with husked rice.

All that morning the clan sisters of the candidates beat the morung gong. The candidates were taken to the forest by the older boys of the morung and instructed in the making of new mallets for the gong. As soon as they returned to the village, they rushed to the gong house and beat the gong with the newly carved mallets. In the meantime the lower jaws of the sacrificial pigs had been cleaned and fastened between split bamboos. The descendant of the village founder then "fed" the pig's jaws with a mixture of rice and ashes, and prayed that the men of Chi and Totok, both powerful neighbors of Wakching, should come and eat.

The intention of this magical formula was not to induce men of these villages to come as guests to Wakching, but to effect the capture of their heads, which would then be "fed" with rice as the pig's jaws had been fed with rice by Yonglong.

Next Yonglong killed a small chicken and let the blood drip on the pig's jaws, and after this the candidates were instructed how to feed the jawbones with rice and ashes. After this they rushed off shouting and swinging small, pointed bamboo sticks. They ran down the steep path near their morung and then threw their miniature "spears" at a large tree near the village spring. Then they returned to the village and, assisted by a few older boys, beat the wooden gong in the rhythm used for announcing the bringing in of a captured enemy's head.

That night the newly initiated boys slept in the morung for the first time. They were not allowed to talk to their parents, and an unmarried young man of the morung took care of them. He gave them the food brought by their relatives and then shut them into one of the sleeping compartments.

The whole ceremonial of this initiation, with the allusion to the taking of heads, the symbolic spearing of a tree, and the beating of the morung gong in the head-taking rhythm, suggests that the rites were intended as a symbolic introduction to war and head-hunting. In Wakching, where the boys were initiated at an early age, this appears somewhat premature, but in most of the Thendu villages a boy's entry into the morung took place at the age of about sixteen. In these villages the initiation rites were more elaborate and included sham fights between the candidates. There, the youths went shortly after the ceremony on a raid to earn their face tattoo. Such ceremonial raids were usually innocuous affairs; the entering of hostile land, which involved, of course, a certain risk, was considered sufficient for the purpose.

It is most likely that in Wakching too the ritual connected with a boy's admission to the morung was originally a real initiation into the life of a warrior. Yet, far from being a mere survival of more warlike times, it continued to mark the entrance of a boy into the economic life of the morung community. All those who had entered the morung at the same time constituted an age group the members of which cooperated in many tasks. The boys of such an age group did not address each other by name nor by the appropriate kinship term, but with the special term *shimba*. The newly initiated boys had to perform certain services for the senior boys, such as fetching water and wood. Those who were slack in this fagging risked being beaten, but in practice it was rare for a smaller boy to be punished by his seniors.

After initiation boys ate most of their meals in their parents' house and used the morung mainly as a dormitory and club. Nevertheless, with entry into the morung a boy's daily routine changed drastically. While previously he had spent his days with his playmates in the village or accompanied his parents to their fields, where he helped them by doing light work, he was now the member of an organized gang, which had its definite function in the economic life of the village. When after the first monsoon showers the overgrown paths had to be cleared, the task of removing the growth and repairing the paths fell to the labor gangs of the morung, and several age groups would work for hours with hoes and *dao*. At the time of building a house or rebuilding a morung the boys of that morung carried bamboos and palm leaves, and did most of the thatching. Messages to friendly neighboring villages had to be carried by junior boys, who usually went on such errands in twos or threes. Above all, however, the labor gangs of the morung were employed in cultivation. They worked not only on the morung fields but went by rote to work on the fields of the gang members' parents. Wealthy men could hire such a gang, and the wages earned belonged to the gang as a whole and were used for the purchase of supplies for celebrations.

Gradually and imperceptibly, a boy was thus absorbed into the life of the adults. He accompanied the older men when they went hunting or fishing, and learned, thereby all that a Konyak had to know. Every few years a new group of boys would enter the morung, and the senior boys helped in their education and were entitled to their services. At the age of thirteen or fourteen a boy would have his chest tattooed, but no ceremony was connected with this operation, which was invariably performed by women of Ang class.

Until marriage a youth was a member of two distinct social units, his parental household and his age group. In the household of his parents he found his food and general maintenance, and it was to this unit that he owed most of his labor. In the men's house and in his age group he strove for social recognition and popularity among the village youth. Although he spent the greater part of his time working with his age group, this effort was not lost to his family. As a member of a gang of ten, he would work for nine days on the fields of others, but on the tenth day the whole gang would work on the fields of his father, possibly achieving more on that one day than a single boy helping his parents could have achieved in ten days.

A conflict between the interests of the two units, family and morung community, could arise only if there was too heavy a demand for work for the morung. If tasks such as the building of a new morung were unduly extended and a morung was short of able-bodied men, the work on individual fields might suffer, but community tasks were usually undertaken during the slack periods of the agricultural year.

What the morung was for the boys, the *yo* or girls' dormitory was for the adolescent girls. There was, however, no common initiation ceremony for girls of one age, but a small family feast was held when a girl of seven or eight had her legs tattooed. Gradually, the girls of roughly similar age would begin to cooperate in informal groups, which developed into labor gangs on the model of those of the boys. Thus, the girls too were drawn away from the family and trained to work for the community. Until she moved into the house of her husband, a girl spent a large part of the day working with her agemates. Only daily household chores, such as fetching water and husking rice, were performed by girls for their own families.

Undoubtedly, adolescent girls bore a greater burden of work than boys of the same age, and the duties of daughters within the parental household were more onerous than those of a son. Girls, nevertheless, enjoyed a fair measure of personal freedom, and their behavior was not subject to restrictive discipline. Yet, the duties and work of women were so closely regulated by routine that even a lazy girl had little chance of shirking the more troublesome domestic tasks, and there was no Konyak girl whose upbringing failed to train her in the duties required of a housewife.

Premarital Sexual Relations and Betrothal

Before reaching puberty boys and girls took little notice of each other, and only brothers and sisters were sometimes seen together, but as soon as young people began to develop an interest in the opposite sex, their attitude changed radically. In public they still maintained a certain reserve, but there were numerous occasions when boys and girls could meet in an atmosphere free of the restraint demanded by etiquette.

Yet, not all the young people of a Konyak village were potential sexual partners. The rules of exogamy, which prohibited marital unions between members of the same clan and ward, applied also to premarital love-making. In Wakching, which consisted of five wards each with its own morung, the wards were grouped together in wider exogamous units. Thus, all the people of the Oukheang and Thepong considered themselves as agnatic kin, and a similar "brother" relationship prevailed among the inhabitants of the Balang and Bala ward. The Ang-ban, however, formed an exogamous unit without affiliation to any other ward. Consequently, a young man of the Oukheang morung had to find his partners among the girls of the Balang, Bala, and Ang-ban, whereas a man of the Ang-ban could choose among the girls of the other four wards. We shall see presently that there were special relations of reciprocity between the Oukheang and the Balang, on the one hand, and between the Thepong and Bala, on the other, whereas the Ang-ban stood outside the system of preferential intermarriage, demonstrated in the figure on page 72.

The system of morung exogamy not only regulated marriage but also determined the attitude of individuals to other members of the village community. A young man of the Oukheang talked to the girls of the Balang or Bala in a tone quite different from that which he used when speaking to girls of the Oukheang and Thepong. When talking to the latter, whom he considered his classificatory sisters, he spoke with considerable restraint and avoided all allusions to sexual matters. With girls who were his potential lovers and wives, however, he conversed in a free and easy manner, and some of the jokes permissible in this context were of an unambiguously sexual nature. Though the girls of his own ward would live in the neighboring houses and, as friends of his sisters would go in and out of

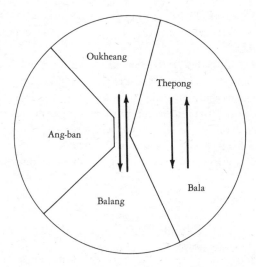

his parental house, he would pay little attention to them and confine his conversation to a few factual remarks regarding the work in house and field.

The traditional companions of a boy of the Oukheang morung were the girls of the Balang and, to a lesser degree, those of the Bala and Ang-ban. At the age of fifteen or sixteen he would begin to accompany his older morung friends on their visits to the girls' dormitories (*yo*) of these wards. At first he would sit rather timidly next to his friends, but soon he would begin to join in the chanting and to talk to the youngest of the girls. Such young girls came only for a few hours to the girls' dormitory, and then they went modestly back to their parents' houses. The younger boys too had no other choice but to return to their morung and to go to sleep there.

Not until a boy was about seventeen did he pursue amorous adventures. His first approaches to a girl were prescribed by etiquette. Late at night he would creep up to the house where the girl of his choice was sleeping, be it a *yo* or a private house (see the previous discussion, Chapter 1, in the section "Community Houses"). There he would gently knock on the wall, and if the girl, noticing the noise, came out, he would immediately pose the stereotyped question: "Will you accept my presents or will you not?"

This question alluded to the small gifts often exchanged by lovers, and if the girl liked him she would reply: "Yes, I shall accept them," and might add, "Tomorrow I shall meet you."

Content with this preliminary success, the boy would return to his morung, and the girl would slip back into the house, but chance did not always favor a boy. Another girl might answer the knocking, and then he would have to beg her to send out the girl he was seeking. If the boy was not to the girl's liking, she would openly reject his advances, possibly pretending that she had already accepted another boy's gifts. If a boy was excessively timid, he might recoil from the risk of an open refusal, and send one of the small boys of the morung to inquire whether his visit would be welcome.

If in one or other way he had obtained the girl's agreement, he returned next evening. Though a love affair was not a matter to be ashamed of, he would cover his head with his cloak lest he were recognized. Again he knocked on the wall, and when the girl came out, they sat down on the platform outside the house, exchanged pan leaves and betel, and talked in low voices. If the girl was still very young and shy, many weeks passed in such innocent meetings in the open, but ultimately the suitor would persuade the girl to retire with him into the dark porch of the house. If the girl, as one of my informants put it, "refused with her mouth, though she consented in her heart," the young man might be bold enough to drag her into the porch and it was there, on a small bamboo bench, that the first intercourse would take place. The lovers were not afraid of being detected by the girl's parents, but to be seen by the girl's brother was considered embarrassing.

Once the lovers knew each other better, the girl would agree to spend the whole night with her boyfriend. The ideal places for such prolonged meetings were the sheltered verandas of the granaries on the outskirts of the village. There, couples of lovers could remain undisturbed until morning, and the owners of granaries favored such use, which protected the stored grain from thieves, and added, in Konyak belief, to the fertility of the seed grain.

At cock's crow the couples parted. The girls crept back to their parents' houses, where they were soon busy husking rice and carrying water. The boys were less energetic. They returned to the morung to sleep.

As soon as a boy had attained a girl's favors, he hastened to present his gifts. Such gifts were not a matter of individual imagination and generosity, but were strictly regulated by etiquette. According to custom, a boy had to give a girl five small bamboo combs, and in return he received from her a small blue cloth such as men wear apronlike tucked into their belts. Other gifts would follow these first exchanges. Of little intrinsic value but great symbolic significance, they marked the beginning of a relationship which involve the reciprocal rendering of services.

During the long months when the rice fields had to be weeded, the girls would ask their boyfriends to help them with this monotonous task, and in response to such a request, two or three Oukheang boys would work with a gang of Balang girls on the fields of one of the girls' fathers.

When at dusk the villagers returned from the fields, the girls would gather on large bamboo platforms outside the village. There, they were joined by the boys of the morung with which they had the closest reciprocal relations. The same young people who during the day behaved with perfect decorum now abandoned all reticence, and many a couple would sit closely pressed together under a single cloak. This was the time when the boys and girls sang improvised alternative chants. The point of these chants lay in the quick and witty repartee, with which a singer capped a partner's last phrase. The language used in this type of competition was a poetic language which differed from that used in everyday speech.

The mutual entertainment of boys and girls at the end of the weeding season has been discussed previously (in Chapter 1, the section "Land Tenure and Agriculture"), and at the Ou-nie-bu, the feast at the beginning of the harvest, the girls baked breads and gave them to the boys with whom they had worked on the fields. The special relationship between Oukheang and Balang, on the one hand, and between Thepong and Bala, on the other, did not exclude friendships and later marriage between Oukheang boys and Bala girls. For although the Bala girls were the traditional partners of the Thepong boys, there was nothing to prevent them from bestowing their favors on boys of the Oukheang or Ang-ban.

Before marriage boys and girls enjoyed complete sexual freedom, and as long as the rules of morung and clan exogamy were observed, no one interfered with the love affairs of young people. Although parents sometimes arranged early marriages, an attempt to forbid their unmarried daughter a friendship with a particular boy would have aroused general disapproval. The institution of girls' dormitories, moreover, made parental control impracticable, and in Wakching it was generally accepted that a girl would have sexual relations before marriage. Virginity was neither valued nor expected of a young girl.

One might assume that under these circumstances most girls would soon have found themselves pregnant, but despite the Konyak's ignorance of contraceptive devices, most girls indulged in sexual intercourse for several years without becoming pregnant. This phenomenon, common among primitive people, has been attributed to the period of relatively low fertility between the menarche and the attainment of full maturity.[1]

The love-making of boys and girls involved no obligations on either side but if two young people had been lovers for some time and had become fond of each other, they began to consider marriage. Usually, it was the boy who took the initiative and asked the girl whether she was willing to become his wife. If a girl did not relish the prospect of marrying her lover, or feared opposition on the part of her parents, she would refuse his proposal and shelter behind the authority of her father and mother. A girl determined to hold on to her lover, however, could usually get her way, or, in the last resort, elope with him to a friendly village.

Once the boy and girl were agreed, the boy asked an older man of his clan to act as go-between and obtain the consent of the girls' parents. Through this go-between he sent them a spear and an arm ring, and if these gifts were accepted, the young couple were considered betrothed. Sometimes betrothals were arranged by the parents at a time when the boy and girl were still immature, and in such cases the boy's father sent the arm ring and spear to the girl's parents. Since every marriage involved the establishment of economic ties between the two families, wealthy people had an interest in finding spouses of equally wealthy background for their children. Yet, the predilections of the young often confounded such plans, and boys and girls betrothed in childhood could break their engagements and marry partners of their own choice. Although cross-cousins

---

[1] See M. F. Ashley-Montague. "Infertility of the Unmarried in Primitive Society." *Oceania*, Vol. 8 (1937) pp. 15–26.

were considered suitable mates, and a man could marry both his mother's brother's and his father's sister's daughter, concrete cases of cross-cousin marriages were few.

In the case of betrothals arranged by the parents there was often a great age difference between the prospective spouses. Thus, I knew a very pretty Balang girl of about eighteen who was engaged to a boy of the Oukheang morung aged about eleven. This betrothal did not condemn her to a life of continence, however, for she was free to indulge in love affairs with the older boys of the Oukheang, Thepong, and Ang-ban, and if one of them wanted to marry her the earlier engagement could be dissolved without much difficulty. If the prospective spouses were adult, a betrothal did not last very long, and the wedding ceremonies followed soon after the partners and their parents had reached agreement.

In some of the villages of the Thenkoh group the sexual freedom of the unmarried was even greater than in Wakching. In the small village of Chingtang, for instance, the girls slept in the many dark cubicles of their dormitory with numerous boys in succession. I was told that in the total darkness of the dormitory a girl sometimes failed to recognize the boy with whom she was sleeping and, hence, if pregnant she could not name the child's father. A girl in this position would hold onto any young man who was making love to her, and, by shouting for the assistance of her friends, force him to reveal his identity. A youth caught thus in the act was held responsible for the paternity of the unborn child and had either to marry the girl or pay her parents one pig and one field as compensation. Clever girls tried to catch particularly wealthy boys in this manner.

Among the Konyaks of the Thendu group, the relations between the unmarried were subject to some rules unknown in Wakching. In Oting, for instance, it was left to a girl's parents to decide when the time had come for her to take a lover. Until then she wore leaden earrings, and this was a signal to the village boys that she was not yet ready for amorous adventures. Nevertheless, a boy might discretely inquire from her parents whether he would be acceptable as a suitor. If they indicated consent, he would occasionally give small gifts to his prospective bride. Although he was considered her betrothed, he was not yet supposed to sleep with the girl. Only when she was seventeen or eighteen would her parents allow her to exchange her leaden earrings for earrings of brass. At the same time her father partitioned off a small room, and there she received her lovers. If she was already betrothed, she was expected to reserve her favors for her fiancé, but even an uncommitted girl was not supposed to change her lovers too often or to have love affairs with two young men simultaneously. Fleeting adventures with guests from other villages were not disapproved of, for such entertainment of guests was considered part of hospitality.

If a girl wearing leaden earrings had a secret love affair and was unlucky enough to become pregnant, her parents would give her earrings of brass, and public opinion would exert pressure on her lover to marry her.

Though in Thendu villages there was probably less promiscuity among the unmarried than in Wakching, and many marriages of chiefs' daughters were contracted as political alliances and arranged by the parents, girls were not expected to remain virgins until they were married. A song, which I recorded in Niaunu in 1962, reflects the attitude of young people to premarital love affairs. It is an alternating chant, sung by boys and girls on the occasion of the nocturnal visits paid by a group of boys to a house where their girlfriends had collected. In an abbreviated form it runs as follows:

Boys: We have come to your house to sing,
Tell us frankly whether you want us as your lovers;
Do not tease us, by saying one thing,
And doing another.

Girls: Alas, we can only love you for a few months,
For we are betrothed to our cousins,[1]
And it would be wicked to break the engagement.

Boys: We do not want to be your lovers
For a short time only;
We want to have you for all time
As our wives.

Girls: We cannot be your wives,
Our parents would be cross with us
If we did so.

Boys: We have offered to become your husbands,
But you want only temporary lovers;
So we shall go to other girls' houses.

Girls: Well, go ahead and make love to them.
If you can get other girls,
We too can get other lovers.

Boys: At first you talked very sweetly,
But now you have turned us down
And we feel very bitter.
We will not waste our time with you,
But go in search of other girls.

Girls: We did not know that you wanted to marry us,
We thought you only wanted to love us.
You never told us what was in your mind.
We were quite willing to make love to you
For a few months, but we cannot be your wives.
For we are already betrothed to our cousins
And they would feel bad if we broke the engagement.
Our mother's brother would beat us,
And we are afraid of him.

Boys: Be it so. We love you all too much,
And if you do not want to marry us,
Let us be your lovers for some time.

This song shows clearly that love affairs not leading to marriage were normal experiences in a girl's life, even though she might have been betrothed to a cross-cousin. The song highlights a girl's willingness to enjoy such premarital adventures without committing herself to a more permanent union, and suggests that young men were keener on marriage than were the girls.

---

[1] Literally: "mother's brother's sons."

Marriage

Though a Konyak boy might have slept with the same girl for many months, no legal obligations resulted from their relationship until the performance of the ceremonies which alone gave social recognition to a couple's union. Not sexual union, which often preceded the wedding, but the acceptance of reciprocal social and economic obligations by the families of bride and groom constituted the basis of a marriage. So important was the economic factor, that even non-consummation of a marriage did not detract from its validity as long as both sides had fulfilled their economic obligations.

We have noted already that in a village such as Wakching the choice of spouses was mainly determined by a system of large exogamous units standing in traditional marriage relations to other similar units within the same village. The link between such units can be regarded as a relationship of permanent affinity.

The ceremonies connected with the conclusion of a marriage are best demonstrated by describing a concrete case. Metlou, a young man of Bala morung and Leunok clan, had had a love affair with a girl of Oukheang ward, but in deference to her father's wishes she married the son of her father's sister, who belonged to the Balang morung, the traditional partner of the Oukheang. Metlou, however, was not discouraged from courting another girl of the Oukheang and gained the affections of Shuidzing, daughter of Weikok of Khoknok clan. To this union the parents of both parties offered no objection. While the decision to marry was taken by the prospective spouses, the bride price had to be negotiated between the girl's father and the boy's go-between. Yoyong, a cousin of Metlou and a member of the great house of his clan, acted for Metlou, and it was he who first approached Weikok in order to arrange the details of the marriage. He took Weikok a spear and a woman's brass armring and, after accepting these gifts, Weikok sacrificed a chicken. Praying for the success of the marriage, he scrutinized the intestines of the chicken and discovered that the omens were favorable. He tied some large leaves to the mainpost of his house, sprinkled them with the blood of the chicken, and invoked the blessing of Gawang, the sky god.

When negotiations were concluded, Weikok made gifts to the go-between, presenting Yoyong with the sacrificial chicken, some cooked rice, and a small basket of uncooked rice.

Three days later the wedding took place. At sunset the go-between took the agreed but modest bride price to the bride's father. It consisted of three brass plates such as Konyaks use for ceremonial payments and one *dao*. Wealthier people paid bride prices composed of a large assortment of valuables and commodities, such as five brass plates, twenty spears, several baskets of rice, chilies and betel nuts, and a few chickens.

The bride's father slaughtered another fowl and gave it to the go-between. Accompanied by her mother, her sisters, those of her brothers who had established independent households, and her father's brother, as well as kinsmen, kinswomen, and girlfriends, the bride went in procession to the groom's house. The bride's father and those brothers who still lived in the parental house were not permitted by custom to participate in this part of the wedding celebrations. This compulsory absence of the men of the bride's household is not easy to interpret, and the Konyaks provided no explanation.

The groom gave to the bride's father's younger brother a bundle of spears to be distributed among the young men of the bride's clan. When all guests had gathered, the groom's parents served the bride with rice and rice beer. After she had eaten, the other guests were offered rice beer and betel, but no solid food.

Subsequently, Yoyong, the go-between, took a small chicken and, touching the bride's hair with it, invoked Gawang, the sky god. He prayed that the bride should be as fertile as a ficus tree and live to a ripe old age. He strangled the chicken and placed it beside the mainpost of the house as an offering to Gawang.

While the men squatted round the hearth, the bride and the girls of her age group withdrew to sit on the rice-pounding table. That night the bride with her company of girls returned to sleep in her parent's house, and the groom spent the night in his morung. On subsequent nights the newly wedded couple slept in a granary in the manner of unmarried lovers. Both continued to live in their parental houses and seldom met during the day.

Several months after the wedding the young wife went to her husband's house to have her legs and knees tattooed with the pattern appropriate to married women. An elderly woman of chiefly status performed this painful operation with the assistance of several girls of the young wife's natal clan, one of whom stayed with the patient for the night to tend her tattoo wounds. Neither the husband nor any other young man was allowed to be present, but after sunset young girls of the husband's clan assembled for a small feast and spent most of the night singing and chanting.

Next day the young wife, whose knees and legs were still sore, was carried home by her father's brother, a service for which the young husband gave him two sides of bacon.

Even when the young wife wore the tattoo marks of a married woman, she did not go to live in her husband's house, but remained with her parents. During this period she led a life hardly distinguishable from that of an unmarried girl. As before, she worked with the labor gang of her girlfriends and in her parents' household, and only occasionally did she help her husband's family with the work on their fields.

Metlou's marriage did not last long. He and Shuidzing had not been lovers before their wedding; it was an open secret that she had had an affair with a man of Maibang clan and Bala morung, and that her first child, a boy called Louming, was her lover's son. Yet, as the child was born while Shuidzing was married to Metlou, the latter was regarded as the child's father and the boy belonged to the Leunok and not to the Maibang clan. Immediately after the birth of her child, Shuidzing moved into Metlou's house, and, subsequently, she bore him a daughter, who died in infancy.

While Metlou was living with Shuidzing in their newly built marital home, he had a love affair with Meniu of Khoknok clan and Thepong morung, the wife of Weiku of Dzonok clan and Bala morung. From an earlier lover she had a daughter, after whose birth she had moved into Weiku's house, but she had had no sexual relations with her husband, who was little more than a boy. When Meniu's daughter died, she returned to her parents' house, and it was at that time that Metlou became her lover.

Shuidzing knew of the affair and often threatened Meniu, saying that she would tear her earlobes, a favorite action of jealous wives, and in view of the large, heavy earrings worn by Konyak women, a threat easily carried out. In the meantime Meniu became pregnant again, and this time by Metlou, but Metlou could not marry Meniu and claim the child without offending the men of his own morung, which was also the morung of Weiku. But he divorced Shuidzing, and paid her father the heavy compensation of two fields, eight brass plates, and one pig. Shuidzing returned to her parents' house, taking her son Louming with her. Later, she married an immigrant from Chi village and kept her son.

As Metlou could not marry Meniu, he married a girl of the Ang-ban morung. But she died before the tattoo ceremony had been performed and never moved to his house. In the same month Weiku died, and now Metlou could marry Meniu. On the night that she gave birth to Metlou's child in her parents' house, she moved, as was customary, to her husband's house.

The confusing network of love affairs and marriages reflected in Metlou's marital history was typical of the behavior of many of Wakching's young people, and formed, indeed, part of the marriage system. Married couples who had not been lovers before the wedding tended to delay consummation of the marriage, particularly if one of the spouses was very young at the time of the wedding. If a marriage had been arranged by the parents, and the spouses had little affection for each other at the time of the wedding, it often happened that husband and wife continued their old lives without paying much attention to each other. The young husband as well as his wife went their separate ways and found love and sexual enjoyment outside marriage. As long as a young wife did not live in her husband's house, no blame was attached to such escapades, nor was the husband expected to be faithful. A man, who resented his young wife's infidelity could, no doubt, forbid her to consort with other men, and if, subsequently, he caught her in the arms of a lover, he could beat them both, but this was his only redress. If he had complained to the girl's father, threatening divorce and claiming the return of the bride price, he would have encountered little sympathy and even risked being accused of wanting to be rid of his wife because he had found a girl he liked better. A young husband in this position usually preferred to remain silent and counter his wife's unfaithfulness with adventures of his own. Only if a wife's lover wanted to marry her had the husband the right to claim a refund of the bride price from him. The position of a wife was more favorable. Though she had no redress if faced with her husband's infidelities, nothing prevented her from dissolving a first marriage if she found another man who was prepared to marry her and compensate her husband.

Indeed, early marriages arranged by parents for their immature sons and daughters involved little hardship because, as a rule, they could be easily dissolved, and it was rare for a marriage to last if there was no affection between the spouses. The possibility of dissolving an unsatisfactory union existed, but the character and temperament of the individual determined whether a man would put up with an unloved partner in the interest of good relations between two families linked by previous affinal ties or whether he was prepared to face the expense of a divorce in order to gain his freedom. The wealthier the families concerned, the greater was the pressure exerted in favor of the maintenance of a marriage alliance involving important economic interests.

Most marriages which survived the period when the spouses lived in the houses of their respective parents were based on mutual affection. Since most couples knew each other intimately before the enactment of the formal marriage ceremonies, this is hardly surprising, for marriages were not usually concluded in the first flush of a passionate attachment, nor did material factors unduly sway the partners in their decision to marry. The camaraderie and complete equality prevailing among unmarried boys and girls persisted in the tenor of the relationship between spouses. For a girl who had for years been accustomed to act independently and had learned to handle the approaches of boys and young men in the girls' dormitory would not be likely to submit to a husband's domination. Those who have observed the Konyaks at work in house and field, at leisure, and at feasts and rituals must have realized that in most practical matters women were the equals of men. Within the sphere of her household a wife operated freely, and as the needs of the household were the focus of family economy, a woman's influence on economic decisions was considerable.

A clear division of labor between the two sexes favored the mutual respect of men and women. The husband was recognized as the head of the family and the owner of the marital home, for the house stood on a site belonging to his lineage, within the limits of his ward, and his clansmen had helped in its construction. It was his duty to maintain the house and the granaries and to provide or replace the furnishings. He produced or purchased all wooden and metal implements as well as all the baskets required in the household. The wife prepared and cooked the food and wove all textiles not purchased from other villages. Just as a man owned his weapons and working implements, so a woman had her personal cooking utensils, looms, and textiles. While the husband concerned himself with the cultivation and storage of rice, the wife was responsible for the planting, harvesting, and drying of taro.

In the absence of her husband a woman acted as head of the house. She received and entertained guests, and if a friend of her husband arrived unexpectedly from another village, she could ask him to stay overnight and await her husband's return. Though hostess and guest would, as a matter of course, both sleep in the main room of the house, this situation aroused no adverse comment. In the presence of the husband too, the entertainment of guests fell mainly to the wife, who poured the beer and distributed betel.

Inside the house spouses conversed in an easy and friendly tone, but outside their own home they showed a marked reserve both in speech and in behavior. Men and women often left the village separately and met only on the fields where they worked together. In public married couples avoided gestures or words of endearment, and this restraint was all the more marked because unmarried boys and girls showed much less reticence. Newly married couples were particularly shy and inhibited in front of others.

The reserve observed by spouses was also expressed in the terms of address. While a young man addressed all the girls who were his partners and potential mates by name, he never called his wife by name, even though she belonged to precisely the same category of girls. Until she had become a mother, he had, indeed, no way of addressing her directly, but once she had born a child, either his own or that of a previous lover, he addressed her as "mother of so-and-so," and she in turn addressed him as "father of so-and-so." This custom of teknonymy was confined to Wakching and the neighboring villages, whereas in Longkhai and other villages of the Thendu group spouses addressed each other by name.

The reluctance of Wakching men to pronounce a wife's name stood in striking contrast to the willingness of most boys to relate their love affairs and to refer to past and current mistresses by name.

The reserve maintained in public by married couples lessened with the years, and middle-aged spouses seemed to be at ease even in front of strangers. Despite the lack of demonstrative endearments, many couples were obviously united by strong ties of affection and loyalty. There were several men who had refused to banish their leprosy-smitten wives and continued to live side by side with an ailing spouse. Similarly, there were husbands of barren women who had resigned themselves to childlessness rather than separate from a cherished wife.

The need to divorce one wife before being able to marry another related only to men of commoner status. For them, monogamy was obligatory, while men of chiefly clan could be married simultaneously to two or more wives. In Wakching there was at the time of my stay only one polygamous marriage, but several of the men of chiefly clan had had two wives, and the chief Chinkak had had three.

In the villages of the Thendu group polygamy was more usual, and most ruling chiefs had a great number of wives. For wives of chiefly class very large bride prices were paid. The chief of Longkhai, who was by no means one of the wealthiest chiefs of great Ang class, paid for the daughter of the Ang of Chi a price of twenty *dao*, sixty spears, two large pigs, two baskets of betel leaves, one large basket of salt, seven chickens, and one goat. For wives of commoner status chiefs paid much smaller bride prices, and some chiefs were accustomed to take commoner girls into their house without formality.

The marriage customs of the commoner clans of the Thendu group varied from village to village. Longkhai commoners were allowed only one wife, but in Oting and Shiong even men of commoner clans could have two wives.

Divorce, Adultery, and Illegitimacy

For those men who were permitted only one wife, childlessness was a common cause for divorce, but neither husband nor wife was required to produce specific reasons for breaking up a marriage, and mutual incompatibility was considered sufficient cause for a parting of ways. Harsh or cruel treatment by either spouse was rare, and in the many case histories of broken marriages which I gathered I heard of only one, apparently psychopathic husband who was reported to have hit his wife. That this was regarded as monstrous by other Konyaks speaks for the rarity of cruel behavior on the part of husbands; such an action would have drawn an immediate response from the wife's kinsmen, who were linked with the husband through the many reciprocal obligations created by the marriage. The backing a wife expected from her natal kin was considered an important factor in the stablization of a marriage, and the parents of a girl wedded to a man of a village other than their own were accustomed to seek out a friend in that village and request him to take the young wife under his protection. In the event of a dispute or if the girl was divorced by her husband, the man standing *in loco parentis* received the fine and compensation which was normally payable to a divorced woman's father. Such a guardian was chosen from among the men of clans which stood to the husband's clan in affinal relations, that is, men who could have become the husband's father-in-law.

In marriages contracted between partners who had had sexual relations either before the performance of the wedding rites or before the wife moved into the husband's house, the first child, which a mother bore in her parental home, was likely to be the offspring of her legal husband, but marriage was not always the outcome of a love affair. It was not unusual for two young people married on the initiative of parents to evince little interest in each other. If after a few months or even years a young wife became pregnant from a man other than her husband, the child belonged, nevertheless, to her legal spouse. The biological father could claim the child only if he decided to marry its mother and compensated the husband by repaying the bride price. If a lover was either unwilling or unable to do this, the wife was compelled to move with her child to the house of her wedded husband, who was not entitled to refuse her admittance. A husband unwilling to keep his wife and her child could divorce her, but if he did, he had to pay substantial compensation to her parents.

Nevertheless, a child born to a wedded woman belonged to the clan of her husband, and the son of a divorced woman, though perhaps raised in the house of his maternal grandparents or that of his mother's brother, ultimately entered the legal father's morung.

More often than not a husband whose wife gave birth to a first child fathered by another accepted the situation with good grace and, even though the identity of the biological father was known, treated the child as his own. The biological father was expected to pay no attention to his natural offspring and the child suffered neither disadvantage nor stigma. In the house of the legal father it had full rights of inheritance and was no less privileged than younger and legitimate brothers and sisters. Consequently, many a man belonged to a clan and morung other than that of his biological father, but as biological and legal father were necessarily of clans and morungs maintaining connubial relations with those of the mother, no difficulty arose over the regulation of marriage.

The comparative indifference to a child's biological paternity was understandable among the Konyags of Wakching, where status differences were not of great importance. However, a similar attitude prevailed among the people of the Thendu group, and even the Wanchus, whose powerful chiefs form a highly privileged group, maintained that not only girls of commoner status but also the daughters of "great" chiefs engaged or married to a chief of another village were free to indulge in casual love affairs in their natal village; a pregnancy resulting from extramarital intercourse was not considered a cause for divorce or the breaking of an engagement which linked two chiefly families. My stay among the Wanchus in 1962 was too brief for the collection of many case histories, but the fact that my informants emphasized the embarrassment caused by the pregnancy of a chief's daughter who was neither married nor betrothed confirms that the pregnancy of high-born girls who were betrothed was considered less unfortunate. Little attention appeared to have been paid to the likelihood that premarital or extramarital love affairs of girls of great chiefs clan would lead, through the birth of natural offspring, to a diminishment of the purity of the chiefly line. The "social" paternity assured by a suitable marriage overruled the question of "biological" paternity, which was conveniently ignored.

As the girls of all groups of Konyaks were accustomed to marry between the ages of fifteen and eighteen, the birth of a child lacking a legal father was not a frequent occurrence. Girls who were neither betrothed nor married occasionally became pregnant, but their lovers were usually willing to marry them, particularly if the parents made concessions in the matter of the bride price. Moreover, there were always some impecunious men anxious to obtain a wife, and such men were usually prepared to marry a girl made pregnant by a lover unwilling to wed her. No social stigma was attached to a wife whose marriage had been contracted in such circumstances.

Nearly all girls succeeded in securing legal fathers for their children. In the 249 houses of Wakching there was, at the time of my fieldwork, not a single child without a legal father. If an unmarried girl bore the child of a married man who was unwilling to divorce his wife, the child was reared in the girl's natal home and the child's biological father paid the girl's parents compensation to the value of one brass plate. A boy born into such circumstances moved, after some years, to his father's house, where he was regarded as a fully privileged member of his father's clan and entered the morung like any other boy.

The fathering of children outside wedlock was no serious consideration. One young man of Wakching, who had married a girl of the neighboring village of Chingtang, but whose bride had not yet joined him, diverted himself with casual love affairs. Asked whether he was not apprehensive of the amount of compensation he would be asked to pay if he made one of his girl friends pregnant, he replied with typical Konyak frankness: "To sleep with a girl is enjoyable, and what does it matter if I have to pay a brass plate?"

From the foregoing one might conclude that Konyaks were relatively free of jealousy. They were tolerant of sexual experimentation among those not yet established as married couples dwelling under one roof, but exclusive relationships were preferred both before and after marriage. It was rare for a boy to engage in two love affairs simultaneously, and a girl discovering a lover's unfaithfulness was likely to break the connection. A married woman learning of her husband's attachment to another woman would approach her rival and ask her to renounce the man. If her plea failed and the affair continued, a jealous wife might attack her rival and, with the help of friends, wrench out her earrings, thereby lacerating the lobes. Public opinion usually sided with the wronged wife, and she was not punished for the injuries she had inflicted on her rival. Similarly, the cuckolded husband of a wife already dwelling in his house was within his rights if he beat her lover.

The adultery of a wife already established in her husband's household was considered a more serious matter than the flightiness of a newly married bride living with her parents. As soon as a couple had founded a household of their own, both spouses were expected to be faithful to each other. From that moment every breach of the marital code was considered an offense against the recognized social order. Though such a lapse did not seriously damage a man's social standing, the ideal was undoubtedly a marriage in which both spouses remained faithful to each other. If we consider the wife's entry into the husband's house as the effective beginning of a marriage, this ideal was often attained. By that time a woman had had several years of sexual freedom, and further temptations were few because the sexually aggressive unmarried men found sufficient scope for adventures among the young girls. A married man too developed other interests than love affairs once he had taken his bride into his house, for as a householder he had to devote most of his energy to the cultivation of his land and the maintenance of his family. If satisfactorily married, husbands felt little inclination for extramarital escapades, and even men who had not found much happiness in marriage told me that they found it difficult to win the favors of young girls, because such girls were monopolized by the unmarried boys who were their work, song, and dance partners.

Marital fidelity was also sustained by a belief in supernatural sanctions. Gawang, the sky god, withheld sons from men who deceived their wives and slept with other women. Similar consequences resulted from a wife's adultery. Thus, it was said that the senior wife of the Ang of Longkhai had no sons because she had had a love affair with her husband's half-brother.

In Niaunu and the neighboring Wanchu villages, which are ruled by autocratic chiefs, the attitude toward the adultery of a commoner's wife differed from the reaction to the infidelity of a chief's wife. A commoner had no legal redress if his wife committed adultery, and her lover could take her into his house without having to pay compensation to the duped husband. A husband, however, who divorced his wife had to pay her parents compensation to the value of one average-sized field. The same applied to women of intermediate class and even those of small Ang status. No fines were imposed in the event of their infidelity. Women married to a chief of great Ang status, however, were subject to a stricter code. Their adultery could place their life as well as that of their lovers' in jeopardy. The father of the present chief of Niaunu had two of his commoner wives as well as their lovers drowned in punishment for their infidelity. Even a chief's wife of great Ang status would have been executed by drowning if caught in adultery. Such punishment was, however, liable to result in feuding between the two chiefly houses originally united by marriage, for the guilty wife's kinsmen felt free to avenge their kinswoman's death, even though they might not have approved of her conduct.

The Marital Affairs of a Wakching Family

While the exogamy of wards and clans channelled marriage into a set pattern of affinal relationships, there remained within this over-all framework considerable latitude for individual choice and the gratification of emotional urges. The following account of the marital complications experienced by two generations of a wealthy Wakching family illustrates both the socially accepted norms and the ways in which individuals contrived to manipulate and at times circumvent them in order to attain their own ends.

A few months before my arrival in Wakching, Shouba, the richest and most influential man of the village had died, and it was his eldest son, Shankok, who became my closest friend among the Konyaks. Shouba belonged to the Khoknok clan of the Thepong morung, and was thus of commoner status. His parents had not been wealthy, but by unrelenting work and skill in trade he had gradually achieved great prosperity. Trade was then very lucrative, because the people of Wakching had begun to purchase manufactured goods in the markets of the plains, and bartered them at great profit to the Konyaks of the interior hills, who at that time were not yet in the habit of traveling far from the security of their villages. Shouba employed the profits from these trade transactions in the purchase of land, and when he died, his holdings were the largest in Wakching.

Shouba's first marriage was childless, and as he was not greatly attached to his wife, he began a love affair with Shongna of Meta clan and Balang ward. Shongna was already married to a man of Ang ward, but she was still living in her parents' house. When she became pregnant, she knew that her child was Shouba's, but according to custom, she had to enter her legal husband's house as soon as she had delivered the child. For a short time she and her infant son, Shankok, lived there, and Shankok was, consequently considered a member of the Ang ward, but Shouba, who was a man of strong character, said to himself, "Shall my son grow up as the child of another man? That must not be." As a commoner, he could not have two wives, and so he divorced his first wife and that night took Shongna and Shankok to his house. To both his first wife and to Shongna's husband he paid large compensations, to the latter twenty brass plates. According to local custom, he had to pull down his old house and build a new one in which to start his new life with Shongna. Subsequently, she bore him four more sons and two daughters. When I knew Shongna she was a dignified woman of comparatively youthful appearance. Shankok stood very much in awe of her, and though nominally he was the head of the family and organized the work of cultivation, it was his mother who ruled in the house.

Shouba's unusual action shows that although in general Konyaks recognized only social paternity, sentiment resulting from biological paternity could on occasion prove a powerful motivation. It would seem that it was this sentiment and not primarily love for Shongna which induced Shouba to abduct her from her husband. Had his affection to Shongna been the main motive, it would have been simpler to compensate her husband and marry her before the birth of her child, and this course would have been much more in accord with usual practice.

Although Shouba had himself followed sentiment, he showed little understanding for the likes and dislikes of his son Shankok. He married his son at an early age to the daughter of one of his friends, a rich man of the Bala morung. The girl, whose name was also Shongna, was at that time adult, and her father hesitated to give his consent to the marriage, fearing that Shankok might want to marry a younger girl when he grew up, but Shouba assured him that as long as he lived he would never permit Shankok to divorce Shongna. Moreover, he contracted on Shankok's behalf to pay a very high compensation in the event of divorce. So the wedding ceremony was concluded, but Shankok was much too young to consummate the marriage. As was customary in such cases, Shongna had a love affair with another man of the Thepong morung, and even when after the birth of a child she entered her husband's house, she continued this connection and gave birth to a second child fathered by her lover.

When at last Shankok was old enough to begin his married life with Shongna, he refused to have anything to do with her. He could not openly rebel against his strong-willed father, in whose house both he and his wife lived, but he decided to boycott the unwanted marriage. Not only did he make no attempt to consummate the union, but he ignored his wife and led the life of a bachelor. When Shankok was about thirty his father died, and although he became head of the household, his attitude to Shongna remained unchanged; he continued to sleep in the morung or found bedfellows among the young girls.

At the time of my arrival in Wakching Shankok was having a very happy love affair with Shikna, a girl of the Balang ward. Shikna was married to Dzingen of Ang ward, but she had not yet taken up her marital life. She and Shankok were very much in love and spent every night together in a granary. From previous girlfriends Shankok already had two children, both of whom were recognized as the children of their mothers' legitimate husbands and lived in the latters' houses. Unfortunately for Shankok, Shikna soon became pregnant, and that meant that she would soon have to enter her husband's house, and thus be lost to Shankok. The thought of the impending separation greatly distressed him. He could have emulated his father's example, divorced his wife, and married Shikna, but his domineering mother opposed such a course and declared that she would not share the house with another daughter-in-law. Moreover, Shankok feared the exorbitant demands of Shongna's kinsmen, to whom he would have had to pay two large fields and ten brass plates if he divorced his wife, and he knew that Shikna's husband would also demand heavy compensation. Though he could easily have met all these demands, he could not face the public discussions and the reproach that he squandered the family's wealth for the sake of a woman. Though Shankok was well liked, his treatment of Shongna and her small daughter, whom, like her mother, he consistently ignored, had already aroused criticism. A man of stronger character might have braved his family's opposition as well as adverse public opinion, and ended the marriage which existed only in name, but Shankok lacked resolution and when, in May 1937, Shikna bore a son and had to enter her husband's house, Shankok was for many weeks in a state of deep depression. He spent sleepless nights in the morung and complained that never again would he find a girlfriend such as Shikna: "No other girl will ever understand me as she did. Whatever she said, I understood, and my words easily entered her mind; like father and son, like brothers we spoke to each other; what could I say to another girl?"

Such utterances show that in a love affair Konyaks sought not only sexual satisfaction; harmony and understanding between lovers were of as much importance as physical attraction. Shikna was not particularly pretty, and I knew a girl of exceptional beauty whom Shankok had abandoned when he began to court Shikna.

Subsequently, he often complained that several children of his were growing up in other men's houses, while the only surviving child of his wife, who lived in his house as his daughter, was the child of another man.

Economic Obligations between Affines

The picture of Konyak marriage so far drawn is still incomplete. Apart from the sentimental attachment between husband and wife in a happy marriage, and the cooperation between spouses living under one roof, there were also obligations involving the kinsmen of both partners. We have seen that at the time of the wedding rites there was an exchange of gifts between the families of groom and bride. This exchange of gifts, additional to the payment of the bride price, inaugurated a series of reciprocal services and presentations which extended over the whole span of married life.

In the course of this exchange of gifts, a man received at the time of every spring festival presents of meat, rice, and rice beer from the nearest agnatic kinsman of his wife. The obligation to deliver these ceremonial gifts passed from father to son. Thus, Shankok had to make such gifts to the husbands of his two sisters, Liphung and Meniu, both of whom were still childless and, therefore, lived in Shankok's house. At the spring festival, which I attended, Shankok gave to his elder sister's husband one hind leg of a pig, eight sides of bacon, four parcels of cooked rice, and two pots of rice beer.

If one of Shankok sisters' had died, he would have received from her husband, or, if the latter no longer lived, from his closest agnatic kinsman, a death due of one field. The obligation to give presents to his sister's conjugal family terminated with her death only if she died childless. If she left a son, he would have received annual gifts from Shankok, and even a daughter would have had a claim on her mother's brother. For three years after the marriage of a sister's daughter Shankok would have given her presents at the spring festival. In return Shankok was entitled to a death due of one brass plate on the death of his sister's eldest son and to a part of any bride price received for his sister's daughter.

Shankok had also inherited similar obligations from his father. Two half-sisters of Shankok's father's father were then still alive, and both received annual gifts from Shankok. A third sister had died, but left a son, and he too was entitled to receive presents from Shankok. For each of these ceremonial gifts a return present had to be made, but the value of the exchange present was usually not even half that of the initial gift.

The same kinsmen who were entitled to gifts at the spring festival were also entitled to presents at the second great seasonal feast held at the time of the harvest.

The ceremonial exchange of gifts between two families was usually initiated by the large single payment which a new bride's kinsmen made to her husband. Thus, at the end of the rice harvest Shankok slaughtered a large pig and sent it to the house of Shanglou, the husband of his sister Meniu. In addition, he gave Shanglou ten large baskets of rice and a large pot of rice beer. Men of Shankok's clan carried these gifts in solemn procession to Shanglou's house. On this occasion the recipient slaughtered a small pig and entertained Shankok and his clansmen. Both Shankok's and Shanglou's kinsmen ate and drank together in Shanglou's house. Women too took part in the feast, and the only person too shy to join the festivities was Meniu, the sister of Shankok and wife of Shanglou.

This example demonstrates the wide ramifications of the economic obligations between affines, and similar networks of reciprocal obligations were centered on every member of the Wakching village community. Those families who had sought matrimonial relationships in neighboring villages extended such obligations beyond the limits of their own village. The regular exchange of ceremonial gifts tempered to some extent the distinctions between rich and poor. As every man gave according to his means, the poorer families received at the time of feasts a share of the surplus of the rich. The urge to increase personal prestige moved richer men to demonstrate their wealth and generosity, and social ambition became thus the spur to economic effort. Those who had gathered an abundant harvest or had been successful in trade were able to provide animals for slaughter and to give generous presents to their affines. The desire to be regarded as rich and of liberal disposition was an important factor in the distribution of such gifts. Thus, Shankok emphasized what an impression it had made on his neighbors when a whole column of clansmen had carried his gifts to the house of his sister's husband.

The system of ceremonial gift exchange stabilized the cohesion of a village community by creating numerous economic links between individual families, clans, and morungs, and it also served to strengthen the position of a wife in her husband's family, for the gifts received gave her the feeling that she was valued by her natal family and could, if necessary, rely on the support of her agnatic kinsmen.

On the death of a wife, the bereaved husband had to give one field to her nearest male kinsmen. If there were children, he continued to receive ceremonial gifts from his deceased wife's kinsmen. A childless woman, when widowed, returned to her natal family, taking with her only her personal possessions. The deceased husband's kinsmen owed her no maintenance. However, a widow with a son continued to live with him in her late husband's house, farming the land which the boy had inherited. In the event of her remarriage, she had to leave the house, and her son, unless he was very small, would go to live with kinsmen of his father. A widow with small daughters was expected to stay in her husband's house only if it was also inhabited by one of his male relatives, but if the widow's daughters were older, she might remain with them even in the absence of such a kinsmen and utilize the deceased husband's land until such a time as the last of the daughters was married. Then, the widowed mother would move with the daughter to the house of her son-in-law, and her late husband's house and land would be taken over by his closest agnatic kinsmen.

Occasionally, it happened that a widow married her deceased husband's younger brother or one of his close kinsmen, but such a union was a matter of choice, not an obligation, and no additional bride price was required. If a widow married a man of a clan different from that of her late husband, however, the new husband had to pay a small bride price to her father or to her nearest kinsman. The kinsmen of the late husband had no claim on the widow or to any bride price paid for her.

Land never passed in the female line. A man's eldest son inherited his entire holding, but he was obliged to allow his younger brothers the right to cultivate a part of their father's land. Gradually, they would acquire land of their own, and by the time the eldest brother died, younger brothers usually had holdings of their own. As the population was more or less stationary, and some clans shrank or died out, while others increased, there was no great pressure on land. Hence, younger sons did not experience much difficulty in acquiring land of their own for cultivation.

If a man had no sons, his daughters could inherit his moveable property such as ornaments and pigs, but land went to their father's kinsmen. In certain circumstances a daughter was permitted to keep a small part of her father's land, but this she could neither sell nor pass on to her children, and after her death it reverted to her father's kinsmen.

In villages ruled by chiefs the land of a clan which had become extinct in the male line was taken over by the chief. However, it was not considered his personal property; it was available for cultivation by any member of the chief's clan. Commoners cultivating such land had to pay rent to the chief.

Death and Funerary Rites

Konyaks had very clear ideas about the fate that awaited them after death. Old men often spoke without any sign of emotion of their entry into Yimbu, the land of the dead. For their journey they needed their weapons, for on the way to Yimbu they would meet all those men whom they had killed in battle and would have to fight them once more. Life in Yimbu was thought of as similar to life on this earth. The departed cultivated the land, celebrated the annual feasts, married, and had children. People who had been married on earth lived in the land of the dead with their original spouses. Even if a marriage had never been consummated and both spouses had subsequently contracted other marriages, it was the partners of a first marriage who would be rejoined and live together in Yimbu.

Illness was usually attributed to the action of supernatural beings, and seers and shamans were employed to discover the cause of an affliction and placate the spirit or god responsible. Some seers claimed that in their dreams they were able to enter the land of the dead, and if they encountered there a man or woman who was still alive on earth, they knew that that person's soul was already dissociated from its body and that the man or woman concerned would soon die. However, sacrifices to Gawang or to other gods could avert death and lure the truant soul back from the land of the dead.

If all attempts to save a sick man failed and he died, not only the members of his household and his closest kinsmen but also other members of the village community were under an obligation to assist in the disposal of the corpse. This cooperation and the sequence of ritual acts can best be demonstrated by the description of an actual funeral.

Chinyak, a young married man of the Oukheang morung, had died after a long illness. All his livestock had been expended in sacrifices to the sky god and the spirits of the earth and, finally, convinced that his own house was pursued by misfortune, he had moved to the house of a kinsman.

On the morning after Chinyak's death the members of his own age group gathered outside the village and, assisted by their traditional partners, the girls of the Balang and Ang-ban, erected a monument consisting of a bamboo structure and a crudely carved human figure. The girls made two head coverings of fresh leaves, one of which was placed on the wooden figure; the other was taken to the house of mourning to be put on the head of the deceased. When the monument was completed the girls returned in single file to the village, scattering large green leaves as they went. This last act of friendship was always performed by girls who were the potential mates of the departed, but was omitted at funerals of older men.

On the day of the funeral all the men of the Oukheang abstained from work on the fields, but only those women belonging to the deceased's clan observed ritual abstention and remained in the village. The unmarried girls of the Balang and Ang-ban, both former partners of the deceased, also observed a day's abstention from work.

All morning the dead body of Chinyak lay in the house in which he had died; men of the Oukheang morung built a corpse platform close to the rear veranda of Chinyak's own house; Chinyak's widow, his mother, and his sisters sat wailing close to the corpse. Singly and in small groups clansmen and friends of the dead man entered the house, bringing betel leaves and small gifts of food, which were later tied to the funerary platform. Among the mourners were men as well as women and, as they left the house, they dipped a finger into a bamboo vessel filled with water, which had been specifically placed in front of the dead man's house for the purpose of this ritual purification.

One of the deceased's sister was married in a neighboring village, and she as well as her husband came to the funeral, bringing the traditional gift of a cloth with which to cover the corpse.

In the early afternoon the three eldest men of the Oukheang morung entered the house of mourning, carrying a bamboo bier. One of them sacrificed a chicken, saying to the dead man, "This fowl, which like you will be eaten by worms, is now your companion; do not look behind at your daughters and kinsmen." Before the corpse was placed on the bier, and taken out of the house, the deceased was once more addressed in a loud voice: "Enter the land of the dead boldly; do not be afraid. If you are asked who you are answer: 'I am Chinyak, son of Yongmek.' "

These words were repeated several times. The wailing increased and the sound of buffalo horns mingled with the lamentations. An old man of Chinyak's clan, wearing the dead man's ceremonial headdress and carrying his spear and *dao*, left the house, and he was followed by the bier, which was carried by four old and completely naked men. Relatives and friends as well as the young men of the Oukheang and the girls of Balang and Ang-ban followed the bier, and the procession moved to the house which Chinyak had left in the last days of his illness.

It was customary to erect a corpse platform either on the communal funerary ground of the clan, which lay just outside the village, or on the deceased's own land, close to his house. In this case the platform was put on Chinyak's land, allegedly because he had purchased it himself and had neither son, nor father, nor brothers to utilize the site. Three years after Chinyak's death his clansmen would sell the land and divide the price.

The bier was placed on the platform and the old men covered the body with a cloth and palm leaves. Then they tied small packets of food onto the platform.

After a few minutes the mourners dispersed, but as long as the deceased's head remained on the platform, the members of his household had to bring it food offerings at the usual meal times.

In the heat of summer decomposition set in rapidly, and even on the day after the funeral the platform was surrounded by swarms of flies. The smell of putrifying flesh pervaded the neighboring houses, and the inhabitants, by no means immune to such a stench, complained that they could hardly bring themselves to eat their food.

Six days after the funeral the head of the corpse was wrenched from the body, and old men and women of the deceased's family had the task of cleaning the skull and removing the remains of the putrefying brain. The skull was placed in an urn hollowed from a block of sandstone, which stood among similar urns on the edge of the village, close to one of the main paths. For three years after death, the skull was given shares of food and beer whenever the kinsmen of the deceased celebrated a feast. This feeding of the skull was done by those members of the dead man's family who lived in the house he had inhabited, that is, by the father or mother of a young man or by the children of an older person. Whoever performed this act of piety addressed the deceased, begging him to eat of the food and to bear no resentment to the living.

No attention was paid to the other bones, which gradually fell to the ground as the bamboo platform disintegrated. Jungle growth soon covered the remains, and no one cared if now and then a pig nosed out the odd bone. According to Konyak belief, it was only the skull to which a portion of a dead man's soul substance continued to adhere, even though his personality had long since completed the journey to the land of the dead.

While the dead of commoner status were put on bamboo biers, those of chiefly class were placed in canoe-shaped wooden coffins the ends of which were decorated with life-sized carvings of hornbill heads. The platform which supported such a coffin was erected in the same place near the chief's house where the stones which marked the capture of heads stood. The chief's body was laid naked in the coffin and a fire was lit near the platform. An old woman, usually of commoner clan, was deputed to watch the body and chase away the flies. When the corpse had sufficiently putrefied, the head was wrenched off and cleaned by old men of chiefly clan. They filled the eye sockets with the white pith of a tree, painted the skull with a pattern similar to the deceased's own tattoo and, using resin, stuck some of his hair to the crown of the skull.

The coffin was covered with palm leaves and laid on a platform outside the village, while the skull was placed in a stone cist and covered with the type of bronze gong which the Konyaks obtained from Burma. For the first year after death the skull was so placed that it overlooked the village path, but later it was turned away from the path.

In some Thendu villages naturalistically carved figures, carrying replicas of weapons and wearing the headdress and ornaments appropriate to chiefs, were placed in front of the funeral platform. These funerary figures were always set up in pairs, one figure representing the chief and the other an attendant.

A variation of the usual funerary customs was found in the Thenkoh village of Namsang. There, the skull, after being wrenched from the body and cleaned, was kept for several months in the house of the family of the deceased. It was set up on a kind of altar and decorated with the ornaments that the deceased had used during his lifetime; whenever the family ate, a small portion of the meal was offered to the skull. At the time of the final disposal, the oldest man of the dead man's morung sacrificed a pig or a cow. Then all the clansmen of the deceased assembled and took the skull to the burial ground of the clan. There, it was put into a stone cist or a pot and covered with a cloth or a stone slab. The officiating elder addressed the deceased for the last time, begging him not to take any of his relatives with him and not to return to his own house. The invocation usually also contained a reference to one of the malevolent spirits living in the earth and believed to be the cause of many deaths.

4

Religious Beliefs and Practices

IN THE MIND OF THE KONYAK the world was made up not only of all the visible objects and creatures of which he had direct sensory experience but also of the multitude of invisible and intangible beings and forces. These entities were imagined as an integral part of the natural order, and Konyaks believed that they were capable of influencing the fate of humans. The Konyak's attitude to invisible beings was basically pragmatic. He gave offerings regularly to the supreme deity credited with beneficent power over men, but as long as life ran smoothly he paid little attention to the numerous spirits of forest and hill. Only when illness or other misfortune struck would he suspect the malevolence of one of the countless spirits and search for a means of propitiation.

The Fate of the Soul

Invisible forces were not conceived as belonging to a world altogether different from the human sphere, and according to Konyak ideology, man himself split at death into several distinct invisible entities. Immediately after the funeral the "soul" (*yaha*), to which a large portion of the individual's personality was attached, set out on a lengthy journey to Yimbu, the land of the dead. The gate to Yimbu was guarded by Doloba, the powerful guardian of the nether world, who questioned the *yaha* before allowing it entrance. Shamans were believed to enter the land of the dead in dreams and trance, and they were credited with the ability to recover and lead back to earth a *yaha* which, straying from a sleeping body, had been kidnapped by some spirit. The absence of a *yaha* from the earthly body, though frequently a cause of serious illness, did not immediately result in death, but its separation from the body could not last longer than a few days if death was not to occur.

Among the Wanchus of Niaunu I found a variation of this belief regarding the soul and the ability of a shaman to follow it into the land of the dead. Here, the success of a shaman's attempts to recapture a soul and lead it back to earth depended on whether he was able to reach the soul before it had crossed a certain bridge. On this bridge, souls were confronted by the guardians of the land of the dead, whom Wanchus called Tsailopa and Tsailonu and imagined as being in the shape of an old man and an old woman. The food and drink provided by the kinsmen of the deceased at the funeral were intended as gifts to these guardians of the nether world. Tsailopa and Tsailonu asked the dead who they were and where they came from. After crossing the bridge the dead arrived at a fork in the road, and those who had died an unnatural death or who had committed many crimes had to take the left path, which was difficult and troublesome, whereas all other souls took the right path. Eventually, both paths converged and led to the nether world, where all the departed lived together.

The Wanchus believed that everything on this earth had a counterpart in the land of the dead. "Below Niaunu," they told me "there is a corresponding village, the Niaunu of the nether world, and below the chief's house there is again a chief's house." However, they added, whereas "there are many chiefs on this earth, there is only one ruler of the nether world."

While at death a *yaha* went to the land of the dead, another part of the personality remained attached to the skull and was capable of benefiting the living in various ways. This soul matter was called *mio* and was entirely distinct from the *yaha*.

In Wakching I watched an incident which illustrates the nature of the *mio*. The Thepong morung was being rebuilt, but the people had been pursued by ill-luck in the ritual hunt which formed part of the building ceremonies. They decided therefore to sacrifice a cock on the skull cist of Shouba, the father of Shankok, who had been the richest member of the Thepong and had died that year. They cast a fishing net over the skull cist in order to catch the *mio* attracted by the sacrifice, and carried the net, believing it held the soul substance, to the morung. When the chase was resumed, an antelope fell to the spears of the hunters and none doubted that this success was due to the beneficial influence exerted by Shouba's *mio*.

The periodic feeding of the skulls of the dead, both those of kinsmen and those of slain enemies, was also indicative of a belief in the power of the soul matter which remained on this earth, while the *yaha* had long settled down to a new life in the next world.

Apart from the *yaha* and the *mio*, there was a third element, which was believed to manifest itself after a man had met a violent death. This was called *hiba*, and can best be translated as "ghost." When a man was killed in war and his head taken by enemies, the members of his morung assembled at night in the house of the deceased and waited for the return of the ghost. On hearing a crackling or a rustling they clapped their hands together as if catching something floating in the air and shouted, *"Hiba, hiba."*

This belief in the return of a dead man's ghost to his own village and house did not conflict with the belief that the *yaha* or soul of those killed in war went to the land of the dead.

Head-Hunting Rites

The idea that powerful magical forces adhering to the human skull could be manipulated for the benefit of the living explains not only the care bestowed on the skulls of deceased kinsmen, but, to a large extent, the practice of acquiring heads of strangers, either by capture or by slaughter of human victims procured by purchase. Though we are hardly justified in assuming that the only motivation of so widespread a practice as head-hunting was the desire to acquire the fertility-promoting force of human blood and the power emanating from human skulls, there can be little doubt that, at least among the Naga tribes, this belief was an effective incentive to the hunting of heads. The quest for prestige gained by successful head-hunters and the desire to avenge the losses of one's own clan or village by killing enemies and capturing their heads were certainly additional motives, but they do not explain all of the ritual associated with the bringing in and disposal of a head trophy.

While head-hunting cannot be considered simply as a concomitant of tribal warfare, the wish to capture heads seems to have been the cause of many feuds between villages which had otherwise no conflicting interests. Konyaks did not normally go to war to enlarge their territory or to loot their opponents. True, there were cases of chiefs expanding their domain by attacking and subjugating a smaller village (see previous discussion, Chapter 3, in the section "Chiefs and Commoners for an example of such action), but most villages coexisted for genera-tions without disputing the boundaries separating their territories, and periods of peace, intermarriage, and a limited barter trade alternated with times when the neighbors faced each other as enemies, each side eager to capture heads if the opportunity arose. Even then there were few large-scale battles or attacks, but after an incident, sparked perhaps by a dispute over the breakup of a marriage between a chief and his wife belonging to another ruling house, there would be ambushes on lone villagers venturing too close to hostile territory or perhaps an assault on a fishing or hunting party.

Only in exceptional cases did warriors set out on a raid with the intention of wiping out an opposing village. The main aim of raiding was the capture of heads, and when the score of those gained and lost was more or less even, negotiations tended to lead to the re-establishment of peace. The only gains of such a period of warfare, extending perhaps over five or six years, were the heads captured by each side. They were carefully preserved and fed with rice beer at all feasts. There was the definite belief that their presence enhanced the fertility and prosperity of the village. The sex, age, and status of the victims were of little relevance. Old people, women, and children would be killed as occasion offered, and the capture of their heads earned the slayer hardly less prestige than the killing of armed warriors. Konyaks avoided open fights whenever possible, for to die in battle was considered not a glorious but a disgraceful fate.

Those who were bent on acquiring a head, and with it the rank and tattoo of a head-taker without risking their own lives, could buy slaves which were

Young men of Wakching dressed for a head-hunting dance.

Head-hunting dance on the open space in front of a Wakching morung.

killed in cold blood. In the past the people of Wakching had occasionally bought such slaves from villages further to the south, and some of my informants described concrete instances of such killings which were staged outside the village in simulation of an ambush.

It is clear that neither vengeance nor animosity had inspired the killing of such victims, and that the only motive had been the desire to acquire the magical virtue attached to a human head, and with it also the right to the insignia of a head-hunter.

At the time of my fieldwork in 1936 and 1937 head-hunting was not permitted in Wakching and the other villages under British administration, but it was still practised in unadministered areas and, through a combination of circumstances described in detail in my book *The Naked Nagas* (1939), I was able to watch head-hunting ceremonies in several villages. I learned then that not all parts of a head were equally valued. The most powerful forces were believed to adhere to the parts around the eyes and to the jaw, whereas the back of the head was of much less potency. This suggests that the connection between skull and soul substance was thought of in very concrete terms, and that a captured head was by no means regarded merely as a symbol of a victory over an enemy. It was the beneficial power which emanated from a human head that the Konyaks were eager to acquire, and little thought was given to any connection between the head and the slain enemy except, as we shall see presently, in the case of men killed in direct retaliation for the killing of a kinsman or covillager. Yet, the heads carried into the village stood in a sense for the slain victims, and in some phases of the ritual they were addressed as if they were persons and capable of exerting an influence on their kinsmen.

When a head was brought back to the captor's village, all the men of the village and in particular all the village elders turned out to welcome the head-hunters. The first rites were performed outside the village on a spot not far from the place where the skulls of dead villagers rested in sandstone cists. There, the captured head was put down and the senior men of all the clans involved in the capture smashed raw eggs on the head, intending by magical means to blind the kinsmen of the dead foe. Then, a clan elder poured rice beer into the mouth and said, "May your mother, may your father, may your elder and younger brothers all come, may they drink our beer and eat our rice and meat. May they all come!" These ritual words were intended to compel the deceased to call his relatives so that they too might fall victims to the spears of the victors.

The senior male of the head-taker's clan carried the head into the village, and if the hands and feet had been cut off and brought in, the younger men carried these in their decorated hip baskets. Next, in procession the men moved to the open space in front of the chief's house and danced for some time; later, the head-takers went to their morung, where women were waiting with bamboo vessels filled with water. With this the young men "washed off" the blood of their enemies, and this ceremonial purification was performed even by those who had not touched enemy blood. The head was placed in a basket and tied, together with the baskets containing additional trophies, to the great log gong. First the young warriors and then the young women beat the gong in the rhythm which announced the capture of a head. Toward evening the captured head was fastened to one of the main posts of the morung, and the warriors danced in the great hall during the night.

The next day all the men of the village dressed in ceremonial clothes and ornaments and painted their bodies and faces with lime. In solemn procession the head was carried either to two stones standing in front of the chief's house or to an upright stone newly set up in a ritual place. There, the senior descendant of the village founder, acting as priest (*niengba*), cut off small pieces of the ears and tongue and called again on the kinsmen of the dead man. He took a small chicken and, sprinkling its blood on the stones, repeated the same incantation. Next, he examined the intestines to see whether the omens were propitious for the slaying of more enemies. The carcass of the chicken was left lying on the stone, but the captured head was taken to a tree close to the morung of the captor and hung up there to dry. Throughout the day there was dancing and feasting, and the whole village observed a day of abstention from work on the fields.

Approximately one month later a great feast was celebrated to mark the final disposal of the head. Many of the prominent men of the morung of the head-taker slaughtered pigs, and after much dancing, drinking, and eating the captured head was taken down from the tree on which it had hung all that month. Once more the head was "fed" with rice and beer, and in doing so the priest intoned the same magical formula which was intended to attract the kinsmen of the victim. Finally, the head was deposited either in the morung or in the ancestral house of the clan of the head-taker.

Some villages, such as Shiong, performed a special rite when a head was taken in retaliation for losses previously suffered. The widow of the avenged man went to meet the successful head-hunters outside the village and thrust a spear into the eyes of the captured head, taunting the victim by reminding him how he had danced in triumph when her husband had been killed. After the head had been brought into the village, the same woman provided a pig for sacrifice in honor of the man who had first wounded the victim. If the village had originally lost several heads, all the widows of those killed speared the captured head and gave pigs for sacrifice, but if only one head had been lost and several taken in revenge, only one pig was sacrificed. In this village the skulls of slain enemies were set up in the chief's house, while the lower jaws were kept in the houses of the head-taker. If the victim had fallen to the spears of several warriors, the skull was divided and each received one piece for storage in his own house or in the ancestral house of his clan.

The Konyaks of Wakching had no very clear idea as to the relationship of a head-taker and the souls of his victim except that on his way to the land of the dead, the head-taker would once more have to fight those he had killed in this life. The Wanchu of Niaunu, however, believed that the victim remained close to his killer until the latter's death, when he would accompany the head-taker to the land of the dead. That the slain became the servant or slave of the slayer was a belief found also among the Ao Nagas and among the Kuki and Chin tribes.

Most Konyaks, however, while they were very conscious of the benefit a community could acquire from the possession of captured heads and the magical power emanating from them, seemed to have little interest in the relation of killer and killed in the next world. To sustain their power and derive from it the highest benefit, all skulls in possession of a village were ceremonially fed at the time of the seasonal feasts.

Konyaks were firmly convinced that the capturing of heads was essential for the well-being of a village and that a community which failed over a period of years to bring in a head would suffer a decline in prosperity. The men of Wakching and other villages of administered territory where Pax Britannica had brought raiding to an end often complained that their inability to capture human heads had resulted in a deterioration of health and general well-being. Their observation was probably accurate, for not only had life lost much of its zest, but increased contacts with the people of the plains had facilitated the spread of epidemics. In the days of head-hunting Naga villages had been very isolated, and as there was little traffic, epidemics seldom affected more than a limited area. With the ban on feuding, however, travel between villages became safer, epidemics spread more widely, and the toll of death from smallpox, dysentery, and cholera was much heavier than the losses sustained in the past as the result of sporadic head-hunting raids.

The Cult of the Sky God

The Konyaks' view of the world of supernatural forces resembled the religious ideas of most other Tibeto-Burman speaking tribes of the hills of northeast India in the sense that they saw their environment as populated by innumerable spirits, partly friendly and partly hostile to man, but controllable by the performance of the appropriate rites. While the many spirits and godlings whom the Konyak propitiated when their help was desired or their unwelcome attentions warded off cannot be dealt with here in detail, it will be rewarding to discuss in some detail the cult of the one deity who stood above all the others and may well be described as dominating the Konyaks' religious ideas.

In the language of Wakching the name of this deity is Gawang and in that of the Wanchu village of Niaunu it is Zangbau. Gawang means literally "Earth-Sky" and Zangbau means "Sky-Earth." Although the emphasis is different, both these names reflect the idea of a universal deity comprising or dominating both spheres of the world. To the Konyaks the name Gawang denoted not the spiritual essence of the universe but a deity of highly personal character associated with the sky more than with the earth.

The people of Wakching imagined Gawang as dwelling in the sky and as having existed before all other beings and things. It was he who created the firmament and who caused the thunder to roll and the lightning to flash. The Konyaks firmly believed that the small neolithic celts which they found occasionally on their fields were the thunderbolts of Gawang. When lightning hit a tree near a village the oldest men sacrificed a chicken and begged Gawang not to harm the settlement.

Konyaks thought of Gawang in anthropomorphic terms, and though his name meant "Earth-Sky," they imagined him in the likeness of a human being of immense size. There was no clear tradition as to Gawang's role in the creation of the world of man, but an old man of Wakching told me, "When Gawang made the earth and men, he made also the rice. We do not know how Gawang made man, but we say that we are his children. If we become rich or poor, it is due to Gawang; if we have plenty of food it comes from Gawang; if we get fever, Gawang has caused it." The latter remark would not have been supported by all Konyaks, for disease and suffering were usually attributed to minor spirits, known as Gashi, who lurked in evil places and would catch passers-by.

At most cardinal events in the life of a Konyak Gawang was invoked. Innumerable were the prayers and incantations by which he was asked to bestow blessings and success on individuals or on the whole community. As a rule, these were brief and simple. Thus, during the wedding ceremonial, when the bride's father sacrificed a chicken, he said only, "Gawang, look upon us kindly and grant us your favor." A little later a kinsman of the groom asked Gawang to grant the bride long life.

When a men's house was rebuilt, an old man prayed, "Gawang, let the men and boys of this morung be healthy." At the spring festival when the clan elders sacrificed pigs, they prayed to Gawang for ample crops of rice and millet, and before a man went hunting he prayed, "Gawang, give that I may encounter wild boars and wild sows." If the hunter was successful, he cut off a small piece of the slain animal's flesh and threw it into the forest for Gawang with the words, "Give me in future another pig."

Gawang was also invoked in daily life. Whenever a Konyak began a meal, he took a few morsels of food and threw them aside with the words, "Gawang, eat you first."

An unusual feature of the beliefs concerning Gawang was the idea that he cared for the moral conduct of men and fulfilled the role of a guardian of the moral order. When I first worked among the Konyaks, I had no experience of other Indian tribes and was not particularly surprised by this aspect of Gawang, but later observations among numerous Indian tribes, including tribes in the eastern Himalayas who resembled Nagas in many respects, made me realize the exceptional nature of a tribal deity so closely linked with the moral order. I even suspected that I might have misinterpreted some of the data relating to Gawang. When in 1962 I spent some time in the villages of the Wanchu group, I paid special attention to this problem and found there a belief in Zangbau ("Sky-Earth"), who was clearly the same deity as Gawang. He too was believed to punish liars and men committing evil deeds by causing their premature death. This tallied exactly with the views expressed by many of my Konyak informants regarding Gawang's concern for human morality. They had often told me that Gawang could see and hear everything human beings did, and that he was angered by breaches of the moral order. This applied even to trivial offenses. Once I asked a young man of chiefly clan whether he, like other boys, would eat from one dish with the girls of commoner status who were his companions in the work on the fields. "Of course, I would like to eat with them too," he replied, "but Gawang sees it." In deference to Gawang he hesitated to break the taboo on eating with girls of lower rank.

Konyaks believed that whoever stole his neighbor's rice or domestic animals, who was unjust and cruel, who beat his covillagers in quarrels, or who bore false witness, incurred the wrath of Gawang. If a man told a blatant lie, one of the bystanders might call out, "You are lying, Gawang sees it and will tear your mouth."

Other offenses as well were punished by Gawang. Men who were unfaithful to their wives and slept secretly with other women were punished by being deprived of male offspring. All Konyaks believed that it was Gawang who bestowed children on people, and to the question why this or that married couple had remained childless, I always received the same answer, "Gawang does not give them any children."

It is a matter of some surprise that Gawang was believed to disapprove of certain customs well established in Naga society. We have seen that Konyaks, though not keeping slaves themselves, occasionally bought slaves and killed them in order to gain head trophies, but some old men of Wakching spoke with great indignation of the villages to the east, where people used "to sell even their own children and kinsmen into slavery." My informants expressed horror at this practice, and emphasized that Gawang became very angry at the selling and killing of slaves and punished the culprits in this life. "Whoever sells a man into slavery or kills such a slave will die early and Gawang will not give him a son to continue his line."

As Gawang punished those guilty of misdeeds, so he rewarded those who excelled in social virtues. Hospitality and generosity were considered highly meritorious, and a rich man of Wakching at whose hearth there was always a place for hungry guests and whose traditional gifts to affines were exceptionally valuable told me that he did not mind spending his wealth in this way because he believed that ultimately Gawang would reward his liberality.

Gawang was also regarded as the guardian of oaths. When two villages decided to terminate a feud and conclude a peace pact, they invoked Gawang, swearing that any who broke the peace and disregarded their solemn oath should meet a speedy death.

Such supernatural sanctions mobilized by the swearing of oaths were the only coercive force which could ensure the maintenance of peace between two autonomous communities, for none of the moral rules which regulated so efficiently relations between kinsmen and covillagers extended to the interaction between different villages, and an appeal to a higher power—in this case Gawang—was necessary if, after a series of raids and counterraids, a state of peaceful coexistence was to be established.

The belief in Gawang as the arbiter of human behavior can perhaps be correlated with the emergence of a sense of public concern with the conduct of individual members of a community, a concern absent in many less well-organized tribal societies. While in a society where conditions are in more or less permanent flux, such as that of the Daflas,[1] individuals can pursue their own ends without being disciplined by public opinion, the Konyaks were bound by a code of behavior enforced by the members of their own in-groups.

Compared to Gawang, the spirits of the earth, the forests, and the rivers were not very important, though at times it was necessary to placate them with offerings of chickens and pigs. Occasionally, ordinary mortals could see the spirits of the wood or of the springs and streams as they slipped by, but only men endowed with special gifts could see Gawang in their dreams, and they described him as a tall Naga with spear and *dao*.

Though Konyaks spent a comparatively large part of their time and resources on ritual activities, and took the performance of sacrifices and the observance of taboos seriously, they did not seem to be open to religious experiences of great emotional impact. There was little room for mysticism in the world view of the Konyaks, and even the seers who could bring about trancelike states appeared as down to earth persons in ordinary daily life. Some claimed that while their body slept, their soul could enter the body of a tiger, and that in the shape of weretigers they had experiences which they remembered in their waking state. According to Konyak belief, the bond between such a man and his tiger familiar was very close, and the death of the tiger was invariably followed by that of his human double. There were sceptics, however, even among Konyaks, and some of my informants ridiculed the pretensions of the men who claimed to be weretigers. Scepticism did not extend to the belief in Gawang and the host of earth-bound spirits, however, and all Konyaks considered their fate to be dependent on the will and actions of invisible beings of whose existence they entertained no doubt.

---

[1] For a discussion of Dafla social controls see my book *Morals and Merit*, London, 1967, pp. 55–73.

5

Present and Future

THE FUTURE OF THE KONYAKS is bound up with the fate of the state of Nagaland, which includes the greater part of the Konyak region. Though forty years ago the Nagas were among the ethnographically best-known tribes of India, today there is no part of the subcontinent about which the outside world has less up-to-date information. In this new state, which comprises the old Naga Hills district and the adjoining "tribal area" of the British period, the government of India has been faced with tribal disaffection and unrest for nearly two decades, but the course of events since 1947 has been so bedeviled by political conflict and propaganda that no one without first-hand experience of the underlying causes of the Nagas' rebellion can assess the situation with any measure of confidence in his own judgment. Without access to official records it is impossible to reconstruct the exact sequence of events which followed the British withdrawal. The Japanese invasion of 1944 had certainly disrupted the previous administration, but the Nagas had, on the whole, proved loyal to the government of India and the British district officers. In the past they had enjoyed a special status and there had been very little interference with their internal affairs. Taxation had been light and the villages had been allowed almost complete self-government. Thus, in 1936 and 1937, when I worked among the Konyaks, not a single administrative or police official was stationed in the Konyak area under British control, and even the visits of touring officials were rare events. Neither were traders from the plains of Assam permitted to enter the Naga Hills. Thus, the traditional pattern of village life had remained largely undisturbed, and except for the ban on head-hunting and intervillage feuds, the administration did not concern itself with the way in which the Konyaks managed village politics.

Traditionally, the inhabitants of the plains of Assam had always avoided entering Naga country, and before the British established their rule over the outer ranges of the Konyak highland, such an attempt would indeed have been suicidal. The Konyaks of the villages in the outer ranges had, however, occasionally descended to the plains and had bartered their produce for such commodities as iron and brass and probably also salt. With the stability and security of travel resulting from the British presence such contacts greatly increased, and whereas government regulations prevented the plains people from entering the hills, increasing numbers of Nagas visited the markets on the edge of the plains. There, they sold mats and baskets, vegetable dyes, and other jungle produce, and occasionally, also poultry and small pigs. In return they obtained metal implements, brass ornaments, glass beads, various textiles, tea, salt, matches, tobacco, and a variety of minor manufactured goods such as umbrellas and a few pieces of cotton clothing. Most important of the economic innovations that resulted from British rule was the introduction of money, and though in 1936 one could still hardly speak of a cash economy, the use of the silver rupee as well as of smaller coins was becoming increasingly common not only for trade with the Assamese but even for some transactions between Konyaks. Thus, rents of fields, prices of animals, ornaments, and articles of clothing as well as certain fines were expressed in money values. The people of villages such as Wakching utilized their easy access to the markets of the plains to develop trade with some of the villages in the interior, whose inhabitants were as yet unaccustomed to venture into the plains and mingle in the markets with tea-garden laborers and Assamese peasants.

The slow growth of contacts between Nagas and plainsmen continued until 1947, when India gained independence and government policy vis-à-vis the Naga hills and other tribal areas came up for revision. An understandable desire to promote the unity of India led to administrative changes aimed at bringing all parts of the country under a uniform system of government. The Naga hills were to be integrated into the state of Assam, and in order to achieve this aim, the regular district administration, involving numerous officials of many different departments, was extended to the previously lightly administered hill tracts. While Assamese and other Indian officials posted in the Naga hills saw themselves as the bearers of a superior civilization and of such benefits as schools and medical care, the Nagas regarded these newcomers as novel rulers who sought to deprive them of the virtual self-government their villages had enjoyed in British days. This prospect dismayed them even more, as none of the Naga tribes had ever been conquered by the Assamese, who had lived in awe of the fierce hill men. Indeed, many Nagas, and particularly the Angamis and Lhotas, who had received a fair amount of education in schools established both by government and by the American Baptist Mission, felt that after the withdrawal of the British, they should be allowed to run their own affairs. After protracted and fruitless negotiations between the government of India and the leaders of the Nagas, hostilities broke out when in 1956 tribal extremists murdered a pro-Indian Naga politician. Troops were dispatched to the Naga hills to restore order, but many of the Naga leaders went underground, and ever since there has been intermittent fighting between the regular Indian army and Naga guerrillas. Unable to suppress the rebellion, the government of India has been prepared to make concessions to Naga national feeling, and in 1957 placed the Naga Hills district and the Tuensang Frontier division, which contained part of the Konyak area, under the Ministry of External Affairs. In 1960 a Naga state, known as Nagaland, was established, and this was to enjoy as high a degree of autonomy as the other states of the

Indian union. However, for an interim period, which has not yet come to an end, responsibility for law and order was vested in the governor of Assam, who acted as governor of Nagaland.

The curtain of secrecy which screens events in Nagaland from the outside world prevents us from understanding why the leaders of the Naga rebellion have felt unable to accept the limited autonomy offered and are continuing to demand full independence and sovereignty. However unrealistic this demand may be, it is symptomatic of the desire of the tribal people to retain their cultural and national identity, even at the expense of material benefits which cooperation with the government of India promises to bring to the area. The demand is unrealistic because in many parts of the Naga hills, though perhaps not in the Konyak region, material and social change has already gone beyond the point of no return, and the continuation of existing services in the sphere of communications, education, and medicine depends on financial support from the central government. It is obvious, however, that the Naga rebels, and with them a section of the Naga population, are convinced that political integration within the Indian union is incompatible with the retention of their cultural characteristics and their own way of life. That they have come to this conclusion is not the fault of the government of India, which has gone a long way in attempting to reach a compromise, and has provided large sums for development projects, but it would seem to be the result of a certain sense of superiority found among orthodox high-caste Hindus, who look down upon the tribals as savages and impure beef-eaters, and do not see anything valuable or worth preserving in Naga culture. This attitude, often adopted by schoolteachers, medical personnel, and minor government officials, must have deeply offended the Nagas, who are a proud and independent warrior people, used to being treated as equals by such British officers as J. H. Hutton and J. P. Mills, who had a profound knowledge of Naga custom and traditions.

It is not possible to assess to what an extent the Konyaks of the villages previously comprised within the Naga Hills district were affected by this development. Being remote from the centers of administration and the activity of politicians, they have never been in the news, and it is likely that their involvement in the struggle between Indian troops and the Naga underground has been only marginal.

A picture totally different from the disturbed conditions in Nagaland is presented by the Tirap district. This district borders on the Konyak area and includes some 23,395 Wanchus, who are virtually indistinguishable from the Konyaks of the Thendu group and maintain marriage relations with the chiefly houses of some of the principal Thendu villages. Unlike the Naga Hills district, Tirap was never incorporated in the state of Assam, for when British rule drew to an end, this area became part of the North East Frontier Agency, which has always been under the control of the central government. Here, a policy well attuned to the needs and aspirations of the tribesmen was mapped out by a well-known anthropologist, the late Verrier Elwin, who, until his death in 1964, held the appointment of tribal advisor to the administration of the North East Frontier Agency. He inspired the members of the Indian Frontier Administrative Service with a tolerant and sympathetic approach to the culture and way of life of the hill tribes. The effectiveness of his influence was partly due to the wholehearted backing which prime minister Jawaharlal Nehru gave to the policy of preserving as much as possible of the tribesmen's cultural heritage, while at the same time developing their economy and gradually enabling them to come to terms with the modern world.

When I visited the Tirap district in 1962, the beneficial results of this policy were obvious. Complete peace reigned among the tribesmen, and there seemed to be no repercussions of the disturbances in neighboring Nagaland. As in the rest of the North East Frontier Agency, outsiders were not permitted to settle among the tribesmen or even to carry on trade and shopkeeping. Proselytizing activities, whether Christian or Hindu, were also banned, and the members of the administration went out of their way to respect tribal sensibilities. A program of road building had improved communications, and the establishment of trading depots under government control enabled the tribesmen to obtain in their own country many basic commodities which previously they had had to barter in the plains of Assam. As during the monsoon, communications by road were still precarious, airdrops were used to supply the governmental staff stationed in remoter areas, and to stock the trading depots. While I was in the Wanchu village of Niaunu such an airdrop took place, and Wanchus, who a few years before had never seen either an airplane or a wheeled vehicle, took it for granted that bags of salt and parcels of cloth would be dropped from Dakotas, and these they collected and delivered to the trading depot in a businesslike manner.

Methods of cultivation had not yet changed, but medical services had begun to have an impact on infant mortality, and as the Wanchu area is fairly densely populated and virgin forest scarce, problems of overcultivation of the available land, and, hence, erosion, may well be looming on the horizon.

There were as yet no obvious signs of change in the social structure, and the government of the villages was run on traditional lines. The chiefs, though deprived of their power over life and death, still wielded considerable authority, and the differences in the obligations and the privileges of aristocrats and commoners persisted. Schools had been operating for only a few years, and it was too early to say whether primary education would alter the people's attitude to the social order and the class structure.

The Wanchus, it seemed, were not yet conscious of any modifications in the political relations between villages, and paramount chiefs continued to receive tribute from the smaller villages of their domain, but there can be little doubt that with the suppression of warfare, the need for alliances and the protection of small villages will disappear, and that the authority and prestige of powerful chiefs will gradually wane.

The relations between the Wanchus and the officials of the administration seemed to be excellent, and the apparent success of the imaginative policy of the government of India in this area seemed to augur well for the future development of the tribal populations of the North East Frontier Agency.

Appendix

Kinship Terminology[1]

The main features of the Konyak kinship system have already emerged from the foregoing account of the interactions between consanguinous as well as affinal kinsmen. The terms by which they address each other are of unusual simplicity, and so few in number that the same term is used to address persons standing in quite different relationships to the speaker. The basic terms of address and their connotations are as follows:

u-phu: Father's father, mother's father; husband's or wife's father; father or mother's father.

u-phi: Father's mother; mother's mother; husband's or wife's father's mother or mother's mother.

u-bha: Father.

u-niu: Mother; father's wife (in polygamous marriages).

u-gou: Mother's brother; father's sister's husband; wife's father; husband's father.

u-nie: Father's sister; mother's brother's wife; wife's mother; husband's mother.

u-chei: Elder brother; father's brother's son; father's sister's son; mother's brother's son (older than speaker).

u-nia: Elder sister; father's brother's daughter; father's sister's daughter; mother's brother's daughter (older than speaker).

These terms with the prefix *u* are used in address, whereas for purposes of reference the prefix *e* is used with the same root; thus "the father" is *e-bha* and "the elder brother" *e-chei*. With these eight basic terms all the terms of address appropriate to persons older than the speaker and, hence, not addressed by name can be formed. Thus, the father's elder brother is addressed *u-bha-yong* (great father) and the father's younger brother *u-bha-dzui* (small father). A man who has three elder brothers addresses them as *u-chei-yong* (great elder brother), *u-chei-owo* (middle elder brother), and *u-chei-dzui* (small elder brother). All these elder brothers address him by name, for kinship terms are used only when speaking to persons older than the speaker. It is birth order and not genealogical position which is decisive. No older man will address a person younger in years with a kinship term, even if he or she belongs to a generation genealogically senior to his own.

---

[1] This section is written in the present tense as language and relationship terms must have remained largely unchanged.

There are no proper kinship terms for younger siblings or for kin of descending generation. Such relatives are invariably addressed by name, and when referring to them to third persons, the speaker uses the words *naha* (child, son, daughter) or *nau* (younger brother, younger sister) in the appropriate combinations. These terms apply to both sexes, and if it is necessary to specify the sex of a person referred to, the words *netan* (man, male) or *sheko* (woman, female) are used; thus "son" is *netan naha* and "daughter" *sheko naha*.

There are no specific terms of address or reference for "husband" and "wife." Spouses do not address each other except as "father (or mother) of so-and-so," and a man referring to his wife speaks of her as *te-nok sheko* ("woman of my house"), and a wife of her husband as *te-nok netan* ("man of my house").

All these kinship terms are used not only in relation to consanguineous and affinal kin but also in addressing other villagers of appropriate age. Thus, a boy addresses all other boys older than he as *"u-chei,"* irrespective of their clan and morung affiliation; all men of his parents' generation as *u-bha* if belonging to his father's morung group and *u-gou* if belonging to the natal exogamous group of his mother. All men of his grandparents' generation are addressed as *u-phu*. Thus, we see that only in the case of persons one generation senior to the speaker is a difference made between agnates and affines.

The only reciprocal terms of address are those used by persons of the same sex and approximately the same age. All boys who entered their morung at the same time address each other as *shim-ba*, and they use the same term vis-à-vis boys of the same age belonging to another morung of the same exogamous group. The corresponding term of address between boys of intermarrying morung groups is *ning-ba*, and both these terms continue to be used throughout life by adult men. They overrule the proper kinship terms, and parallel cousins of the same age address each other as *shim-ba*, while cross-cousins address each other as *ning-ba*.

Corresponding reciprocal terms are used by girls and women; these call their agemates of the same exogamous group *ou-shim* and those of the intermarrying group *ou-ning*.

These reciprocal terms of address are used not only among persons of the same village but also in conversation with people of friendly neighboring villages. Thus, men of Wakching address the men of similar age of such villages as Wanching, Chingtang, and Tanhai as *shim-ba*, but address as *ning-ba* those whose mothers had come from Wakching, and who are thus equated with affines.

When addressing friends from Thendu villages, Wakching men used the reciprocal term *ei-ba*. This is a loan word from a Thendu dialect in which *ei-ba* is the term of address for a parallel cousin of the same sex.

The only reciprocal form of address used between persons of opposite sex is *a-mai*, and this is used between men and women of different villages, but never between persons of the same village.

The most notable feature of the kinship terminology of Wakching is the absence of any distinction in the terms of address used in respect to persons of the same and of a different exogamous group, with the one exception of the terms relating to the generation immediately senior to that of the speaker. Thus, a girl addresses not only her own elder brother and his agemates of the same exogamous group as *u-chei* but also her mother's brother's son and her potential marriage partners who belong to other wards of the village. She drops this form of address only if the young man in question becomes her lover or her betrothed.

Similarly, the term *u-phu* is used equally when addressing the father's father and the mother's father. The two men must necessarily belong to different clans and morungs, and a man's relationship to his paternal grandfather, from whom he inherits property, and such positions as are hereditary in his lineage, is of a different order from his relationship to his maternal grandfather, who lives in a different ward and, possibly, a different village.

· Thus, we see that the kinship terms reflect social relations and attitudes only to a very limited extent, and it is notable that the Konyak kinship terminology, though it is of classificatory type, is much simpler and less expressive than that of other Naga tribes such as Angamis, Semas, and Aos. However, before drawing any far-reaching conclusions, it would be necessary to record the kinship terms current in Konyak dialects other than that of Wakching, a task which I was not able to complete in the time at my disposal.

Recommended Reading

ELWIN, VERRIER, 1957, *A Philosophy for NEFA*. Shillong, India: NEFA Administration.
A general account of the principles underlying the administrative system of the North East Frontier Agency.
————, 1958, *Myths of the North-East Frontier of India*. Shillong, India: NEFA Administration.
An annotated collection of myths and folk tales of the hill peoples of NEFA.
————, 1959, *The Art of the North East Frontier of India*. Shillong, India: NEFA Administration.
A well-illustrated account of the art and crafts of the tribes of NEFA.
————, 1959, *India's North-East Frontier in the Nineteenth Century*. New York: Oxford University Press.
An anthology of historic accounts on the peoples of the North East Frontier Agency.
FÜRER-HAIMENDORF, C. VON, 1938, The Morung System of the Konyak Nagas, Assam. *Journal of the Royal Anthropological Institute*, 68:349–378.
Partly overlaps with this monograph, but contains additional details.
————, 1939, revised edition 1953, *The Naked Nagas*. London: Methuen; Calcutta: Thacker, Spink & Co. Ltd.
A personal account of fieldwork among the Konyaks and other Naga tribes; partly complementary to this monograph.
————, 1943, The Role of Songs in Konyak culture. *Man in India*, 23:69–82.
A collection and interpretation of Konyak songs.
————, 1955, *Himalayan Barbary*. London: J. Murray.
A travel book describing exploration and anthropological fieldwork in the Subansiri region of NEFA.
————, 1962, *The Apa Tanis and their Neighbours*. London: Routledge.
A more systematic study of the tribes described in *Himalayan Barbary*.
————, 1967, *Morals and Merit*. London: Weidenfeld and Nicolson.
A study of values and social controls in South Asian societies, which contains a section on Konyak attitudes complementary to this monograph.
HUTTON, J. H., 1921, *The Angami Nagas*. London: Macmillan.
————, 1921, *The Sema Nagas*. London: Macmillan.
Two classic studies of important Naga tribes.
LEACH, E. R., 1954, *Political Systems of Highland Burma. A Study of Kachin Social Structure*. London: G. Bell.
Contains a detailed analysis of the contrast between democratic and autocratic systems of tribal government relevant to the understanding of Konyak society.
McCOSH, JOHN, 1837, *Topography of Assam*.
One of the earliest accounts by a European of the Naga tribes.
MILLS, J. P., 1922, *The Lhota Nagas*. London: Macmillan.
A comprehensive study of the Lhotas; the comparative introduction contains ethnographic notes on the Konyaks.
————, 1926, *The Ao Nagas*. London: Macmillan.
An excellent study of the southern neighbors of the Konyaks containing a wealth of detail on material culture and ritual.